To Patricia,

A little glimpse
into the "real me"

All the best,

Kevin LaBuche ☺

Published by CelebrityPress®, Orlando, FL

CelebrityPress® is a registered trademark

Printed in the United States of America.

ISBN: 978-0-9907064-7-2
LCCN: 2014958959

This publication is designed to provide accurate and authoritative information with regard to the subject matter covered. It is sold with the understanding that the publisher is not engaged in rendering legal, accounting, or other professional advice. If legal advice or other expert assistance is required, the services of a competent professional should be sought. The opinions expressed by the authors in this book are not endorsed by Celebrity Press® and are the sole responsibility of the authors rendering the opinion.

Most CelebrityPress® titles are available at special quantity discounts for bulk purchases for sales promotions, premiums, fundraising, and educational use. Special versions or book excerpts can also be created to fit specific needs.

For more information, please write:
CelebrityPress®
520 N. Orlando Ave, Loft #2
Winter Park, FL 32789
or call 1.877.261.4930

Visit us online at: www.CelebrityPressPublishing.com

BOOM!

THE LEADING
ENTREPRENEURS & PROFESSIONALS
REVEAL THEIR SECRETS TO
IMPROVING YOUR
HEALTH, WEALTH & LIFESTYLE
WITH THEIR

EXPLOSIVE
TECHNIQUES

CELEBRITY PRESS®
Winter Park, Florida

CONTENTS

CHAPTER 1

GET READY FOR THE BIG BOOM!
HOW ENTREPRENEURS CAN CREATE
PERPETUAL PROSPERITY FOR ALL

By Mark Victor Hansen 13

CHAPTER 2

THE MAGIC OF MISSIONS

By Nick Nanton & JW Dicks 25

CHAPTER 3

FEEDING THE KIDS IN AMERICA

By Sir Chef Bruno Serato 41

CHAPTER 4

**MASTERMIND GROUP – WHEN 1 + 1
DOES NOT EQUAL 2**

By Arthur Magoulianiti 51

CHAPTER 5

**SECRETS TO BOOMING SUCCESS
IN BUSINESS AND LIFE**

By Christina Skytt 61

CHAPTER 6

**REWEAVING THE FABRIC
OF LIFE AFTER LOSS**

By Donna Farris 73

CHAPTER 7

**WHEN YOU ALMOST DIE,
YOU WAKE UP**

By Fahad Buchh 83

CHAPTER 8

**WHAT IS YOUR BEST STRATEGY
NOW IN 2015 FOR HEALTH
CARE COVERAGE?**

By Frank Saltzburg 91

CHAPTER 9

**IS THERE ANYTHING GOING
ON IN MAY?** — A SIMPLE
QUESTION WITH A
LIFE-CHANGING IMPACT

By Kim LaBreche 101

CHAPTER 10

**YOUR OWN FASHION BRAND
IN 90 DAYS: WALKTHROUGH
FOR HARDCORE GAMERS**

By Julia Antufjew 111

CHAPTER 11

**SALES EXCELLENCE – SEVEN
STEPS TO ACHIEVING
EXTRAORDINARY SUCCESS
IN SALES**

By Richard Tyler 123

CHAPTER 12

**FINANCIAL PILLARS
TO BUILD WEALTH FOR
THE FAMILY**

By Bibi Bunmi Apampa 137

CHAPTER 13

**THE SECRET
TO SUCCESS . . . ?**

By Robert Goldsmith 147

CHAPTER 14

LET IT GO, LET IT GO

By Tom Shieh 159

CHAPTER 15

UNDERSTANDING THAT SUCCESS COMES FROM WHO YOU ARE, NOT WHAT YOU DO

By Greg Rollett 169

CHAPTER 1

GET READY FOR THE BIG BOOM!
HOW ENTREPRENEURS CAN CREATE PERPETUAL PROSPERITY FOR ALL

BY MARK VICTOR HANSEN

BOOM!

That's the sound of disaster – or the sound of success. It can be the sound of an epic collapse – or an epic success. The sound of a mighty enterprise crashing – or an innovative new idea breaking down tired old business-as-usual thinking.

BOOM!

It's a word that sums up our times. In the words of the famous beginning of that book we all had to read in high school, "It was the best of times, it was the worst of times." Charles Dickens could have easily penned those words today, because they're truer now than ever.

BOOM!

A Boom can be an incredibly good thing – or incredibly bad. Which is it for you? Are you shuddering in the corner in anticipation of a horrendous Boom? . . . Or are you eagerly awaiting the blessings of a bountiful Boom?

It, of course, depends on what you're looking at – and who you're listening to. Most importantly, it comes down to: *how you view the world or what your predominant world view is...*

If that view is informed solely by the news media, you may be tempted to never get out of bed in the morning. The media's job is to scare you into staying tuned and they do as good a job as possible at doing just that. If your view is informed by hope, faith, belief in ever greater possibilities, and optimism, by the kinds of folks who want to grab onto visionary leadership that leads to new innovations, ideas, and the new and exciting changes that are in the wind, that's a different story.

Sure we have problems, lots of them. The question is, do we frame those problems from the standpoint of "How do we suffer from them?" Or do we frame them by "How do we *solve* them and get paid exquisitely well for our solutions?" If we choose the latter way of thinking, we can't help but see that big problems contain big opportunities, often in disguise. And consequently, enormous problems have enormous opportunities.

That's why I'm happy to announce some wonderful news: *We have enormous problems! Better yet, we have enormous opportunities that can become omni-profitable.*

And that's why I know in the deepest part of my soul that all of us here on planet Earth have the potential to enter into the biggest (positive) Boom in human history.

For the last 40 years, I've been fortunate enough to be involved with all sorts of businesses – life insurance, real estate, network marketing, medical corporations, as well as my well-known public roles as author and public speaker. And through all these extensive and incredibly varied ventures which continue to this day, I've learned that there is only one answer to the question, "How's business?"

That answer is "Booming!"

The truth of the matter is, business is always booming for *someone* - even if it's not booming for you at the moment. Somewhere, somehow, it's always booming for other individuals, other companies, and yes, even countries. And if it's not booming for you as you're reading this, then let's go back to your choice of how you think about your plight: Do you suffer – or do you solve? If you want to solve, you find the people who are making money in your business, you find out how they're doing well, and then you either do the same thing or something new that's better. You strive to do something remarkable and unique.

You take your enormous problem and find the enormous opportunity in it.

The book business has been my main industry for many years – it's exciting to be able to say I've sold 500 million books, half a billion of them beginning with the original *Chicken Soup for the Soul* volume I wrote with my friend, Jack Canfield. But in 2008, the book business, like a lot of other businesses, went into the tank. Borders went belly-up, along with a lot of other major bookstore players. Today, Barnes and Noble is about all that's left of the chains and even it is teetering on the edge.

But...

E-book Sales? Boom. Amazon sales? As I write this there are new breakthroughs known only to a few people. I can't be sure that they will succeed, but note that Spotify wants to digitally start selling books by the page or chapter for pennies or that POD (Print On Demand) machine, the size of a businessman's desk, may show up in major retailers, like Wal-Mart, and be able to print you whatever book you want in five minutes. That will make a vastly bigger and more inclusive library available than ever before in history to everyone, everywhere, and potentially translated into every language with off-the-shelf software. Boom! Authors can still easily profit if they play the game the way it should be played in this digital age. Books still make money. And luckily, mine are in that category.

Humans are by nature problem-solvers. That's why, for our own good and for the world's as well, we have to widen our lens beyond our own individual difficulties and look at humanity as a whole. When we make that leap, when we dare to take on that kind of Big Picture, we can't help but find once-in-a-millennium opportunities for essential transformation – and explosive prosperity.

THE EQUATION FOR TRANSFORMATION

Enormous opportunities comes from enormous needs – and, right now, there are more people in extreme need around the world than at any other time in human history. Over half the global population is surviving on only one meal a day (if they're lucky), and inadequate clean water that is safe to drink. I've worked in India and China and I've seen the need for myself. Need is also generated by such modern dangers as Ebola and dramatically changing weather patterns, which threaten entire countries in some cases. There have never been more people on the planet – and there have never been greater threats to them.

On the other side, we have incredible potential, more potential than at any other time in human history. We can instantly find out about whatever we want to know about – in the blink of an eye, because, also for the first time in human history, we have instant world communication at our fingertips. More importantly, we also have the exponential technology and tools to meet the world's needs, if we put our minds to it.

So here's the reality check to those who think a huge destructive Boom is all but inevitable: *Positive transformation is more possible than ever before.* A company like Uber can change an entire industry with a simple, powerful idea and a great software app. Suddenly, 50,000 people are put to work by something that didn't exist four years ago. New, strong and lasting brands can be built in a very short time, due to the power of the Internet and the ubiquitous Smartphones that guide us through our daily lives. YouTube ten years ago was just two words that didn't used to belong together; same with Facebook. Now both companies are a part of our everyday language.

Then there's Google, which wasn't even a word at all before its invention a couple of decades ago. It ushered in this new Superbrand culture. Now, everybody in the world knows what Google is all about. Okay, not everybody – because in China, the search engine giant was shut down due to its usage by movements backing the Dalai Lama and Tibet against the government. For that reason, Google was rendered virtually useless by official censorship, shrinking its overall usage from 36% of the Chinese population to just over 1% in no time flat. That, in turn, effectively cut off most citizens of that country from the rest of the world.

Enormous problem. Enormous opportunity.

Jack Ma grew up in China without much education, learning English by watching television. I helped train him as he came to America and instantly saw how businesses were creating profitable and meaningful connections over the Internet. Well, one of those TV shows he watched came in handy – because he named his company "Alibaba," after the famous Arabian Nights tale. In that story, a secret entrance could be opened simply by uttering the phrase, "Open Sesame." Jack's idea was to open his own "secret entrance" to global businesses for the Chinese. He got $1 billion from Yahoo! to create his online portal, and that ended up to be a very good investment - because Yahoo!'s value skyrocketed by $50 billion when Alibaba became a huge sensation (it's now valued at over $200 billion). The day that Jack Ma's dream of Alibaba came true as an Initial Public Offering in New York City, his net worth boomed to $18 billion. Despite the mysticism inherent in the Arabian Nights stories, there was no magic to any of this. Jack was aware of the fact that many affluent Chinese people (there are now over 3 million who are multi-millionaires) wanted to be able to reach out beyond their borders to do business – and he found enormous opportunity in that enormous problem.

When I was in graduate school, I was taught by the legendary Dr. Buckminster Fuller, who gave us his equation for success:
$$RW = I \times E.$$
"RW" stands for Real Wealth, "E" stands for Energy and the "I?" Well, it stands for one of two things: Ideas, Innovation or Invention. In other words, when you combine and multiply an exciting idea for change with the energy to put it into action, the potential wealth you create for yourself and the world is boundless. And if you don't believe him, ask Jack Ma.

It all starts with that all-important "I." The right idea creates an amazing Boom that the entire world can't help but hear. I've given talks on "How to Think Bigger than You Ever Thought You Could Think" – because that's the first step towards achieving a magnificent "I." One person can change the world more easily now than at any other time in history. But if that one person doesn't grant him or herself permission to think that big, the right idea never has a chance to materialize.

Ideas can be unlimited – if we don't limit ourselves. The ideas I put into my best-selling books don't go away. As I said, I've sold 500 million books - but studies show that I've probably had over a billion readers. Books get passed around 3 or 4 times in America, 12 times in India, 50 times in China, because in China there are few book stores and they are all owned, controlled, and censored by the Chinese government. In China, our *Chicken Soup* books are subtitled "An English Sandwich," and have sold 375,000,000. The ideas in my books awaken the soul and spirit of my readers' and keep them alive, interested and wanting to keep learning and growing.

The right ideas never die. The right ideas make a difference, a big booming difference.

FOUR WAYS TO CHANGE THE WORLD

A good Boom or a bad Boom. What will determine which Boom humanity will experience?

I believe there are four areas in which change is required in order to make 100% of humanity physically healthy, and economically and ecologically successful.

1. Energy

My wife, Crystal and I've invested in NPC (Natural Power Concepts and Technologies company in Oahu, Hawaii. With innovative inventions by the world's top Surrealist Artist and the Leonardo of our time, John Pitre, we have innovated the technology to have green, clean sustainable energy for the entire planet now. We have deep ocean current tidal energy technology, that utilizes the endless waves pulsation of 9 to 12 feet a minute converting it into energy. That energy can be converted into kilowatts to run our homes and companies or used to effortlessly and inexpensively desalinate our water or break H2O into usage and saleable hydrogen and oxygen. That's virtually free, unlimited power, once our technology is utilized. When the ocean's energy creates water, that water can create food, and that food can feed the world. The Earth has a fundamental abundance that we can tap into – and when we do, Boom! You suddenly have enough food for everyone and you suddenly have a higher standard of living for everyone, everywhere. It also ends the basic reason for war because there will be no shortage of resources.

I'm also on the board of the world's biggest commercial solar energy company, Principal Energy out of Texas, run by Mike Gordon. We're building giant solar farms that will eventually run our whole country and serve greatly in many solar rich areas of the world. We have to do something - because we're running out of energy. The technology is there – the natural power of the sun and the ocean is there – what's holding us back? Only our old ideas of where energy comes from and entrenched vested interests.

2. Education

Again, new solutions can open up the world to education – and help us all tap into the power of great minds that currently are never properly trained or cultivated.

I'm on the Board of Directors and an investor in the World Education University, which you can find out more about at WEU.org. The basic idea is that, for $25 a month, you have access to a wide range of online educational resources. If you commit to doing it for a year, we'll even send you an iPad. Everyone, regardless of location, nationality or educational status, is welcome to enroll. It's a competency-based university where any student can achieve a degree that is totally acceptable by every university in the world.

This is the kind of program that can raise the level of our global conversation and provide affordable access to a world-class education to those who otherwise might never have had the opportunity.

We have multiple innovations at WEU. One of the most exciting is a Global AA (Associative Arts) Degree. It can be studied in any language and transferred and accepted by every other University in the world.

Our goal is to serve a billion students in the next decade.

3. Healthcare

Again, technology can provide an amazing transformation in this critical area. If we can prevent health problems before they occur, and there's no reason we can't, we'll lower costs and extend life spans.

Right now, I'm wearing a little medallion that could contains my total health history. No matter what doctor I go to, the MD could instantly access all that information, including my family history, and he or she can better understand what problem I might be having. Here again, I'm blessed to be aware of and slightly involved in exciting, leading-edge technology like patches you can wear that can help stimulate health in everything from relieving obesity to chronic discomfort.

Our medical approach has to be preventative – with a prevailing attitude of "Patient Heal Thyself." You've got to be your own doctor and do the right things for your own health. You've got to exercise, you've got to get enough sleep, and you've got to have enough nutrition. These are things you have to study on your own; no one can do it for you. . . anymore than anyone can do your push ups for you. The more we are all well educated on how best to take care of our bodies, minds, and spirits, the better we'll all feel and the more we'll be able to do. After prevention, if we do have a health break down, then we need an integrated medical approach to our bodily restoration.

4. Money

We have to get money circulating again. An entrepreneur takes low value and, like an alchemist, transforms it into high value when bringing it to the marketplace and to the world – creating value and potentially a fortune and dynamically compelling future. That makes everybody better off. That's why I love to work with entrepreneurs, people like Richard Branson at the upper levels and, on the other side of the coin, talented but un-established, beginning innovators who think differently and have the courage to want to positively effect change.

For example, I created a company with Bill Walsh called Mirikel. We built this company by looking at the four companies that were truly excelling in today's market. We looked at what Branson did to build 400 companies to generate $21 billion a year. We then did a 180 and studied the work of Dr. Muhammad Yunus, a Nobel Prize winner who took 100 million women out of poverty in Bangladesh and pioneered micro-financing and microcredit. We looked at iTunes, which does $44 billion a year at a 37% net margin, and has more money invested in the bank than any other company invented by Steve Jobs. And finally, we checked out Uber, whose transformative power I've already discussed.

That led us to the revelation that we wanted to create something that would connect all the great entrepreneurs, famous and unsung, and put money to work in the way I've described. We named our new app "Mirikel" and designed it to empower mobile business entrepreneurship, allowing anyone to join up and do business anywhere they want in the world mobile by telephone. It's a concept we think is so unique, so original, so different that it's going to catch fire. After all, there are 7 billion Smartphones out there. There are more Smartphones than toilets. No one's ever tried to create a unified business platform across all of them. Bill Walsh and I are dreaming that our idea will boom, serve everyone to become telephone entrepreneurs, to the benefit of total humanity. We are, and if it works as planned, we will create a boom, just like the one I hope this inspires you to create.

When we address all four of the above areas in the right way, we can easily create an awesome Boom that will lift us to an exciting new age. I'm trying to do my part, but I'm just one little guy working in a lot of promising new directions. Fortunately, I have an enormous amount of energy; God invested me with great brain power and a great talent - the ability to get along with people who have the right technology and resources, people who look at needs that most are completely ignoring and say, "Hey, wait a second, how do we make this work for everybody, and not just for a few of us?"

It's the mindset we all need to truly transform everything around us. It's time to make the world work for the 100%, not the 1%. It's time to take all of humanity totally out of poverty and into prosperity. Yes, this can be the biggest Boom-time in history. But we've got to wake up, get excited and get to work.

You heard it here first – **Boom!**

About Mark

Mark Victor Hansen is a world-renowned authority in the field of self-development, on story telling and money making for kids and adults. Mark is the co-creator of the best-selling series: *Chicken Soup for the Soul* and *One Minute Millionaire.* He is founder of the Richestkidsacademy. com. He is the winner of the prestigious Horatio Alger Award for Distinguished Americans, that has given over a hundred million in college scholarships to homeless and at-risk students.

Mark has been on over five thousand radio and TV shows, he is the host of the infomercial series called: *The Hansen Report,* seen by over ten million worldwide. Mark has been given ten honorary doctorate awards, including those from Southern Illinois University, University of Toledo, Shanghai International University, etc. He is dedicated to keeping free enterprise free, creating profitable innovations and inventions to get and keep our economy and entrepreneurship rocking.

Having sold over 500 million books, he is the world's number one best selling, non-fiction author, according to *Guinness Book of Records.* Mark is the prolific author of more than three hundred and six books, including fifty-eight New York Times number one bestsellers. Hansen's books have been published in more than forty-four languages.

Mark is popular as an international inspirational speaker because he gets individuals and companies to quickly multiply their results! As a renowned seminar leader, he has an impressive list of having given more than five thousand talks to over six million people, in seventy-eight countries.

Mark also loves inspiring individuals to write and create their own book at his website: wealthywriterswisdom.com.

Mark has deep interests and investments in alternative green, clean, sustainable alternative energy like Natural Power Concepts and Principal Solar—World's Biggest Commercial Solar Company. He is working zealously to create a sustainable economy and ecology that works for one hundred percent of humanity.

As a passionate philanthropist, he has worked to raise money for the American Red Cross, March of Dimes, Habitat for Humanity, Boy Scouts of America and many others.

Mark is happily married to Crystal, with five children and five grandchildren.

CHAPTER 2

THE MAGIC OF MISSIONS

BY NICK NANTON & JW DICKS

A man with money is no match against a man on a mission.
~ Doyle Brunson

The Movie Star was not acting like much of a movie star.

It was a week before Christmas and he had the bright idea, after a few beers, to make a giant batch of his special salad dressing recipe in an old bathtub of his basement. The plan was, after it was mixed and completed, he would then pour the dressing into old wine bottles that he would cork and give away as Christmas presents to his neighbors.

But the Movie Star had a problem. He had nothing big enough with which to effectively stir the huge tub of dressing.

He called upon a close friend to help him out. But when the friend arrived, he saw that the Movie Star had found a way to take care of the problem – and the friend was aghast at the solution.

The Movie Star was stirring the giant tub of salad dressing *with a filthy paddle from his canoe* – a canoe that he kept down by the river that ran alongside his house. When the friend objected, the Movie Star offered his theory that somehow the oil and vinegar in the salad counteracted any problems of hygiene that might crop up from his old and disgusting stirring implement.

After the dressing was completed and after all the designated gift bottles were filled, the Movie Star and his friend couldn't believe just how much salad dressing was left over in the tub. That's when the Movie Star had a great idea...

...why not bottle the rest and sell it through the local stores?

The friend, noting the concoction's unsavory creation, said that was against the law. Rules and regulations for food preparation had to be followed. The Movie Star was undeterred. He enlisted his friend to help him create a real business in which they would sell his salad dressing in supermarkets. The Movie Star would put up the seed money, the friend would do the legwork. Taste and quality would be paramount to the product.

Just as importantly, the profits from the company, should it actually have any, would go exclusively to a mixture of charities – in the words of the Movie Star, "tax-deductible charities and causes, some church-related, others for conservation and ecology and things like that."

From those humble beginnings, the Movie Star, whose name was Paul Newman, launched one of the iconic food brands of our times, *Newman's Own*. Over the past three decades, it's generated $400 million, all of which was given to countless charities. Today, *Newman's Own* produces nearly 100 individual food products.

No doubt much of its success was due to the quality of the offerings and the celebrity of the company's founder. But, in some cases, celebrity names don't help much! Who remembers Frank Sinatra's neckties? Flavor Flav's fried chicken? Jerry Lewis's movie theatres? Hulk Hogan's Pastamania? Kanye West's women's clothing line?

No, there was a big difference when it came to *Newman's Own* – and the late, great Paul Newman absolutely understood what the real appeal of his *Newman's Own* line was. He said, "If you can make people aware that things are going to charity, and if there are two competing products on the shelf, maybe people will grab the one where some good will actually come of it."

He understood the power of a mission.

Imagine going to see a James Bond movie where 007 had nothing to do but some paperwork. Consider turning on an episode of a CSI series in which the stars just had coffee and talked about what they had for dinner the previous night. Or think about tackling a video game where the main character had no reason to go anywhere or do anything.

Pretty boring, right? Not to mention pointless and uninteresting. In all of the above cases, if there isn't some kind of mission involved, nobody's going to care and nobody's going to spend time or money on them. Why bother?

Now, think about *your* business - or your non-profit organization.

We're very sure it has a very big mission in *your* eyes – and that's most likely to bring in money. And we have no problem with that. But what we think you should do is take a look at your business from the *public's* eyes. Why should *they* care? What motivates them to buy from it – or, more importantly in terms of developing a vibrant, strong customer-, client- or donor-base to emotionally engage with it?

That's where having a mission in place can make all the difference. We believe that if you really want to see your organization "Boom!", you should definitely consider becoming Mission-Driven.

In our best-selling book, *StorySelling™: Hollywood Secrets Revealed: How to Sell Without Selling by Telling Your Brand Story,* we presented overwhelming evidence that demonstrated the power of storytelling in marketing and branding. In this chapter, we're going to take that a step further – and show you how to give your organization an incredible ongoing story that will both attract crowds and also keep them at your side for years to come. When you become Mission-Driven, you create a reason to make people root for you – and, even better, do business with you, which they see as a way to support your specific mission. When a business becomes Mission-Driven, it gives itself *a clear and distinct advantage* that its competition lacks. Again, it's all about StorySelling™ (or selling without selling by telling your brand story), and having a Mission-Driven brand story gives you a narrative that's almost irresistible.

How powerful is having the right mission posted in a prominent place at your company? So powerful that *it allows you to break every business rule in the book* – and still be incredibly successful.

For example, you can…

- Give Away Half Your Products
  Tom's Shoes was a 2006 start-up that announced for every pair of shoes it sold, it would donate a pair of shoes to an impoverished child. After the *Los Angeles Times* ran an article about the new company, it was suddenly deluged with online orders that accounted for *nine times* its available stock. Toms is currently valued at over $600 million.

- Tell Customers NOT to Buy from You
  Could anything be crazier than a company taking out a full-page ad asking its customers NOT to buy what it's selling? That's just what clothing retailer Patagonia did in a full-page *New York Times* ad on Black Friday, 2011 – with a headline that boldly announced, "Don't Buy This Jacket!" They did this in order to announce its "Common Threads" Initiative, promoting sustainability over consumerism. In other words, they wanted people to hang on to their clothing longer and lessen their environmental footprints. That campaign, ironically enough, resulted in the company realizing some of its best sales ever.

- Stay Closed on the Busiest Day of the Week
  The national chain Chick-fil-A was founded in 1967 by
  S. Truett Cathy, who recently passed away at the age of 93.
  The most unusual thing about these restaurants has always
  been that none of them ever open on a Sunday – traditionally a
  day when many Americans like to eat out. Cathy's reason for
  that was simple – he was a devout Christian who didn't believe
  in dealing with money on the "Lord's Day." The company
  itself states that, "Cathy believes that being closed on Sunday
  says two important things to people: One, that there must be
  something special about the way Chick-fil-A people view their
  spiritual life and two, that there must be something special
  about how Chick-fil-A feels about its people."[1] Cathy himself
  said, "I feel it's the best business decision I ever made."[2]

In other words, even though the decision to be closed on Sunday
was a genuine belief of Cathy's, he also understood that it sent
out a strong signal to customers and employees alike that Chick-
fil-A was different than, say, McDonalds or a Burger King.
Everything wasn't about making a profit – some things were
actually more important to Chick-fil-A. Fast food places are
not known for their principles – but Chick-fil-A immediately
cut itself apart from that pack by sacrificing at least 14% of its
potential revenue for its values.

THE CORE COMPONENT OF
BEING MISSION-DRIVEN

Being Mission-Driven means you're committed to something
above and beyond "business as usual" – even though your
mission might be all about business. In our last book, we
wrote about how Tony Hsieh (who we've had the privilege to
spend some time with along with a few of our top clients in
our Mastermind group) built the online shoe retailer Zappos into

1. Green, Emma. "Chick-fil-A: Selling Chicken With a Side of God," *The Atlantic*,
   September 8, 2014.

2. Ibid.

a billion dollar business – simply by taking customer service to crazy extremes. 99.9% of other business owners would have seen investing such a high amount of time, energy and money in that arena as a waste of resources. And yet, that kind of counter-intuitive move was what made Zappos such a huge sensation. Their mission of gold-plated customer service was exactly what attracted hordes of customers.

The real secret behind Mission-Driven success can be found in the Bible, more specifically in Luke 6:38, which states: *"Give and it will be given to you."* You might make a substantial sacrifice in the short-term – but, long-term, you will make an incredible gain.

And that goes even if you have to commit THE cardinal business sin – and give away your product.

Is there anyone reading this who hasn't heard of TED talks – the famous innovative and engaging 18-minute presentations given by the world's greatest minds? If you haven't heard of them, you're part of a very small group.

The TED conference was first held in 1984 as a one-off event backed by Silicon Valley; it only became an annual event in 1990. Still, you would have been hard-pressed to find many beyond the conference's participants who knew of its existence back then.

That all began to change big-time in June, 2006. That's when TED made their talks available absolutely free for online viewing. Suddenly, the summit that no one had heard of transformed into one of the most successful media organizations in the world.

As Bruno Giussani, the European director of TED, said in 2012, "We started by giving away our content. But for the last three years, we've been giving away our brand, our methods and our formats."[3] It's a concept they call "Radical Openness" – and, as

---

3. Cadwalladr, Carole. TEDGlobal 2012: "The more you give away the more you get back," *The Observer*, June 23, 2012.

far as they're concerned, no other company or organization in the world has gone as far in opening itself up to the world. What mission drives them?

Giussani provides the answer. "It's clear to everybody that not only are we living in a globalized world, but also an [increasingly complex] world. It's one in which traditional boundaries are breaking down, one after the other. And there are different answers to this. One is that you close. You have protectionism, and borders and tariffs and national preferences. And the other is that you open and facilitate additional changes. So we started looking at whether the world is more open or not. And whether it should be more open.

"We found that, giving stuff away, we received even more in return. We have a huge committed community. A lot of brand recognition. And the capacity to touch communities where we had no contact before. The more you open your processes up… the more you receive in return."

For this nonprofit foundation, that last statement rings incredibly true. By 2009, TED talks had been viewed online 50 million times. In 2011, they hit 500 million views. In 2012? They crossed the magic billion mark.

When you bring your beliefs out into the marketplace in a meaningful way, whether you're a nonprofit like TED that wants to create a more intelligent global conversation, or whether you're simply selling shoes like Toms Shoes or Zappos, it can't help but differentiate yourself from your competition and attract those who are like-minded.

THE FIVE PRIMARY ATTRIBUTES OF A SUCCESSFUL MISSION

With everything in life, there's a catch – and attempting to become successfully Mission-Driven is no different. In this case, how far your mission takes you depends a great deal on (1) what that mission is all about, and (2) how you choose to carry it out.

For example, addressing point (1), if your mission is one that involves strangling kittens, we strongly doubt you'll get much of the public on your side. Conversely, addressing point (2), even if your mission is "pro-kitten," you still will have considerable difficulties if your tactic to help kitties…is to strangle puppies.

You see what we're getting at. You must have in place an admirable purpose – and an admirable way of *fulfilling* that purpose – if your Mission-Driven agenda is really going to have the desirable impact.

With that in mind, we're like to share what we consider to be the Five (5) Primary Attributes of a Successful Mission. Not all of these have to be in place for a mission to be effective – but each one of them contributes a vital ingredient.

Attribute #1: Positivity
Earlier in this chapter, we discussed how staying closed on Sundays benefited Chick-fil-A's Mission-Driven status. It was a positive for them, as they were giving up potential revenue because of their religious principles – they weren't really hurting anyone besides themselves (and yeah, okay, also people who wanted a chicken sandwich on a Sunday).

However, when the public discovered Chick-fil-A contributed millions of dollars to groups advocating against same-sex marriage, suddenly the company's mission was seen as polarizing and divisive. True, half of the country flocked to its side, staging "Chick-fil-A Appreciation Days" and spiking their sales during those individual events – but the other half campaigned loudly and vocally against the company, causing many formerly-loyal customers to boycott the chain for good – and even some communities to block new franchises from opening.

The company bounced back when management finally and fully backed away from injecting personal opinion on social issues into their corporate policy. And that's why current CEO Dan

Cathy told *USA Today* in 2014, "All of us become more wise as time goes by. We sincerely care about all people." Today, the chain is on track to surpass longtime fast-food king McDonalds in overall sales.

The lesson? An organization's mission should always be seen as positive and proactive, and never as punitive or negative. Most of the public does not respond well to that mindset, and the company that employs it risks limiting itself to a small furtive following rather than a broad supportive coalition.

Attribute #2: Relevance
Whatever mission you decide on for your organization should have some meaning to your intended customers, clients or followers. If your mission is to save the sand flea, for example, you probably won't get as much support as you would helping larger social initiatives such as clean water or green energy programs, programs that affect all of us.

Your mission can also be important from a specific service or product standpoint. For example, a food manufacturer who guarantees all its product ingredients are organic or a paper goods company that only uses recyclable ingredients is going to attract customers simply because many of them look for businesses that have these policies in place.

Finally, your mission can be important from the standpoint of your actual business *practices.* On the home page of Southwest Airlines, you'll find their mission very clearly stated: *To connect People to what's important in their lives through friendly, reliable, and low-cost air travel.* Wal-Mart's is even simpler: Deliver the lowest prices possible.

To sum up, your mission should not just be relevant to *you.* It's more important that it's relevant to your audience.

Attribute #3: Effectiveness
The name of the decades-long super-successful TV and movie franchise is *Mission: Impossible* – not *Mission: Incompetent.*

That concept only works as a comedy. You can have the greatest, most important mission in the world – but if you're perceived to be a failure at that mission, it will hurt you as much as it would have helped you if you had been successful at it.

In 2006, Bono put together an all-star line-up to promote Red, a charitable effort designed to channel money to the Global Fund to Fight AIDS, Tuberculosis and Malaria. Steven Spielberg, Oprah Winfrey, Chris Rock and Christy Turlington were just a few of the superstars enlisted to be public faces of the campaign. Corporate support was also high-profile and mammoth – Gap, Apple and Motorola threw in an estimated $100 million to get the word out.

A year later, all that effort resulted in only about $18 million in donations. Worse, it spurred a backlash against Bono and the companies involved in the campaign, who gave to the fund partly based on how many products they sold through the Red initiative. As Ben Davis, an advertising professional, said in 2007, "The Red campaign proposes consumption as the cure to the world's evils. Can't we just focus on the real solution – giving money?"[4]

Attribute #4: Altruism

The Red case study reinforces another necessary element to a successful mission – the perception that you're *not just acting in your own best interests.*

Let's return for a moment to the earlier examples of the TED foundation giving away its content and Patagonia telling people not to buy too much of their clothing. In both cases, these organizations are seemingly shooting themselves in the foot – TED, by offering for free its exclusive intellectual property, and Patagonia, by discouraging customers from buying their product. In both cases, however, the public sees companies that *care more about the common good than their own good* – and

4. Frazier, Mya. "Costly Red Campaign Reaps Meager $18 Million," *Advertising Age*, March 5, 2007.

rewards them for that exemplary behavior.

We all admire the intelligent selfless act – because it seems to happen so rarely. And many of us will then support them for just this reason. In a world where everyone too often seems out to enrich themselves at others' expense, it's refreshing and hopeful to see the opposite behavior in action.

Attribute #5: Engagement
Your mission should also actively cause people to want to be involved with it.

In 2014, the Ice Bucket Challenge took social media by storm – because it was spontaneous (to this date, nobody is sure how it actually started), fun (some of the video bloopers involved were hilarious) and had an altruistic mission (raising money to combat the ALS disease). In just one month, from July 29 to August 29 of 2014, the ALS Association raised $100 million through a simple and virtually-free viral campaign.

Contrast those results with those of the Red campaign we just discussed, where some of the hugest powers-that-be spent countless dollars and time trying to achieve the same effect – and sadly created an extravagant failure (if raising $18 million can rightly be called a failure). In contrast to the Ice Bucket Challenge, Red came across as elitist and mercenary – which, in turn, failed to engage the public at a significant level.

There are many ways that mission engagement can be implemented. The mission could have a direct benefit to a customer (think of Zappos' heightened customer service policies). It could appeal to one's higher instincts (think of Patagonia and TED). Or the organization could simply make it fun to participate (think the Ice Bucket Challenge). We'd like to point out that engagement is one of the most important attributes an organization should have in place. If you can't engage your audience properly, it doesn't really matter how good your mission might be, as Bono discovered to his horror.

If we go back and analyze the mission Paul Newman set out on when he created Newman's Own, we can easily see it had each of the above five attributes in spades.

1. *Positivity* – when you saw Newman's smiling face beaming at you from the product packaging, it had to make you feel good about buying.

2. *Relevance* – Paul Newman was not only one of the biggest movie stars of his time, he was also one of the most respected, as he was known as someone who used his fame sparingly for only projects he thought mattered. In other words, he was a bit of a Mission-Driven Movie Star! When a guy who wouldn't even sign autographs for fans lent his name to a product line, the public was automatically intrigued.

3. *Effectiveness* – his products were well-regarded in terms of quality and taste. More importantly, they quickly earned a lot of money for the charities Newman supported.

4. *Altruism* – all after-tax profits went directly to those charities, meaning Newman didn't pocket a cent from his own super-successful company. (We're not saying you have to give all of your profits away, however, this is a clear illustration that happens to be a great example!)

5. *Engagement* – as noted, the company marketed Newman's involvement in a fun and inviting way. The food itself used as many natural ingredients as possible and the charitable intent was well-publicized. This all added up to create great engagement with consumers.

A Mission-Driven company like *Newman's Own* can't help but succeed – and it really was ahead of its time. Today, research shows Mission-Driven companies have huge advantages in today's marketplace. As a matter of fact, consumers almost expect organizations to be Mission-Driven.

So put the principles of this chapter into practice to fully realize your outfit's mission. You'll be surprised just how loud a "Boom!" you'll make as a result!

About Nick

An Emmy Award Winning Director and Producer, Nick Nanton, Esq., is known as the Top Agent to Celebrity Experts around the world for his role in developing and marketing business and professional experts, through personal branding, media, marketing and PR. Nick is recognized as the nation's leading expert on personal branding as Fast Company Magazine's Expert Blogger on the subject and lectures regularly on the topic at major universities around the world. His book *Celebrity Branding You®*, while an easy and informative read, has also been used as a text book at the University level.

The CEO and Chief StoryTeller at The Dicks + Nanton Celebrity Branding Agency, an international agency with more than 1800 clients in 33 countries, Nick is an award winning director, producer and songwriter who has worked on everything from large scale events to television shows with the likes of Steve Forbes, Brian Tracy, Jack Canfield (*The Secret*, Creator of the *Chicken Soup for the Soul* Series), Michael E. Gerber, Tom Hopkins, Dan Kennedy and many more.

Nick is recognized as one of the top thought-leaders in the business world and has co-authored 30 best-selling books alongside Brian Tracy, Jack Canfield, Dan Kennedy, Dr. Ivan Misner (Founder of BNI), Jay Conrad Levinson (Author of the Guerilla Marketing Series), Super Agent Leigh Steinberg and many others, including the breakthrough hit *Celebrity Branding You!®*.

Nick has led the marketing and PR campaigns that have driven more than 1000 authors to Best-Seller status. Nick has been seen in *USA Today, The Wall Street Journal, Newsweek, BusinessWeek, Inc. Magazine, The New York Times, Entrepreneur® Magazine, Forbes,* FastCompany.com and has appeared on ABC, NBC, CBS, and FOX television affiliates around the country, as well as CNN, FOX News, CNBC, and MSNBC from coast to coast.

Nick is a member of the Florida Bar, holds a JD from the University Of Florida Levin College Of Law, as well as a BSBA in Finance from the University of Florida's Warrington College of Business. Nick is a voting member of The National Academy of Recording Arts & Sciences (NARAS, Home to The GRAMMYs), a member of The National Academy of Television Arts & Sciences (Home to the Emmy Awards), co-founder of the National Academy of Best-Selling Authors, a 16-time Telly Award winner, and spends his spare time working with Young Life, Downtown Credo Orlando, Entrepreneurs International and rooting for the Florida Gators with his wife Kristina and their three children, Brock, Bowen and Addison.

Learn more at: www.NickNanton.com and www.CelebrityBrandingAgency.com

About JW

JW Dicks, Esq., is America's foremost authority on using personal branding for business development. He has created some of the most successful brand and marketing campaigns for business and professional clients to make them the credible celebrity experts in their field and build multi-million dollar businesses using their recognized status.

JW Dicks has started, bought, built, and sold a large number of businesses over his 39-year career and developed a loyal international following as a business attorney, author, speaker, consultant, and business experts' coach. He not only practices what he preaches by using his strategies to build his own businesses, he also applies those same concepts to help clients grow their business or professional practice the ways he does.

JW has been extensively quoted in such national media as *USA Today,* the *Wall Street Journal, Newsweek, Inc.,* Forbes.com, CNBC.com, and *Fortune Small Business.* His television appearances include ABC, NBC, CBS and FOX affiliate stations around the country. He is the resident branding expert for *Fast Company's* internationally syndicated blog and is the publisher of *Celebrity Expert Insider,* a monthly newsletter targeting business and brand building strategies.

JW has written over 22 books, including numerous best-sellers, and has been inducted into the National Academy of Best-Selling Authors. JW is married to Linda, his wife of 39 years, and they have two daughters, two granddaughters and two Yorkies. JW is a 6th generation Floridian and splits his time between his home in Orlando and beach house on the Florida west coast.

CHAPTER 3

FEEDING THE KIDS IN AMERICA

BY SIR CHEF BRUNO SERATO

I didn't realize it at the time, but on April 18, 2005, I launched the organization that would later become known as Caterina's Club. Nine years later, and Caterina's Club feeds dinner to over 1,200 needy children a day in Orange County alone, and has helped 70 families move from motel rooms to apartment complexes. As the President of this charity, I've learned much along the way. It hasn't been in an easy road, but when I take a moment to reflect on this meaningful work and the amount of people – especially children – it has benefited, I know my efforts are worth more than all the time in the world.

I am also aware that many generous people dream of giving back, but they simply don't know where to start. How do they get the word out about their charity? How do they receive funding? What are the rules and regulations they must follow in order to get their organization underway? These are just a few of the questions I hope to answer here. But first, I'd like to share a little about Caterina's Club.

It all started on that day in April that will forever be ingrained in my mind. It was a Monday, and my mother, Caterina, was visiting me from her hometown in Italy. As the owner of the Anaheim White House Restaurant, my days were very busy, and it just so happened that Caterina, whom I affectionately called Mamma, was spending most of her vacation in the restaurant with me. I was also on the Board of the local Boys and Girls Club, and so I invited Mamma to come along for an event. That afternoon, the Boys and Girls Club Director, Mike Baker, was showing Mamma around, and he pointed out a little boy who was eating potato chips from a small bag. This sight didn't seem too unusual until he mentioned that the boy was actually eating his dinner. Potato chips for dinner? Neither Mamma nor I understood until Mike explained that the boy was a *motel kid*. He'd leave the Boys and Girls Club in a few hours and go home to a single room, most likely infested with bugs. He'd spend his night in the darkest environment imaginable, in a place known for its prostitution, gangs, drugs, and pedophiles. And on top of all that? He'd go hungry.

Mamma gave me a little nudge. I leaned over as she whispered that I should feed the boy. As a matter of fact, I should feed *all* of the kids at the Boys and Girls Club, at least for one day. Though Mamma suffered from Parkinson's disease, she and I went back to the restaurant, and working together in the kitchen, made 70 plates of pasta. I could never say no to Mamma.

From that point forward, the charity I named after my mother's selfless example has provided dinner for the kids at the Boys and Girls Club seven days a week, 365 days a year. Though the amount of kids quickly doubled, I was able to maintain the program out of my own pocket until 2008, the year the economy took a hit. Many customers stopped going out to eat and my restaurant lost thirty percent of its business. The kids needing my help continued to increase, and I thought I had no way of financing the program without taking a line of credit out on my house. And so, I did.

Despite the tough times, Caterina's Club continued to receive recognition from all over the country. In 2011, Katie Couric of CBS News interviewed me about our program, and that same year, I was nominated as a Top 10 CNN Hero. In addition to many other recognitions, I received the Pope John XXIII Award for Outstanding Achievement Towards Humanity from the Italian Catholic Federation, the President's Volunteer Service Award from Presidents George W. Bush and Barack Obama, the Celebration of Father's Award on behalf of the Simin Hope Foundation in the company of Andrea Bocelli, and the highest honor possible when I was knighted on behalf of Italy's President, Giorgio Napolitano. By 2011, seven years after the first plate of pasta was served, we received our first donation. It was also during this year that I obtained my first fiscal sponsor.

I had exceeded my mother's expectations of me, but I still felt like I wasn't doing enough for the motel kids. It pleased me to recognize that these children were no longer going home hungry. Instead, they enjoyed a gourmet dinner each evening. What bothered me was the knowledge that even though their stomachs were full, they still had to go back to a motel, the most dismal and dangerous of all places.

In 2011, I decided to expand the efforts of Caterina's Club to help families transition from the motel to an apartment. Motel rooms aren't cheap. Often times, it is cheaper to rent an apartment than it is to reside in a motel room. Most parents also need to spend extra money on take-out meals because a motel room has no kitchen. The problem is that apartment complexes typically charge the first and last month's rent before allowing a family to move in. For families living paycheck to paycheck, this fee often makes the move impossible.

Caterina's Club's newest goal is to pay for these two months rent, allowing more children to live in a healthier environment. Qualifying families must have at least two children, one parent must have a full-time job, and the family must be able to afford the rent for the apartment of their choice. If they can meet these qualifications, then Caterina's Club will facilitate the move. Just to see the faces of these children whose lives have been changed makes me feel proud. I remember checking up on a family of seven that we'd moved into an apartment. The mother and father had lived with their five children in a single motel room for twelve years. Twelve years! When I saw them again, I noticed that the two oldest children – teenagers now – were smiling. I'd never seen them smile before. Not once. They were different kids now that they truly had a place to call home.

It is amazing to observe the amount of people who want to lend a hand in helping Caterina's Club, and also those who have walked in my footsteps and started their own charities to feed children. There are similar programs in Chicago and New York City, both run through Boys and Girls Club facilities. The most remarkable accomplishment for me, however, is that Caterina's Club has served as an example in other countries. Our charity has been showcased on Univision, a Spanish network, and similar organizations have sprung up in Latin America. The host of an Italian cooking show called La Prova del Cuoco, Antonella Clerici, invited me on her show as a guest and revealed that she was going to start a program with the goal of feeding Italian kids.

You may feel inspired to feed children, or you may have a completely different vision. You may wish to reach out to troubled youth, to save abused animals, or to award those who've made major accomplishments academically or in their communities. Whatever you are passionate about, you can begin a charity, just like I did. There are many things I would have done differently if I had to do it over again. For example, I would have obtained a fiscal sponsor sooner. For this reason, I have come up with seven steps to help you begin your charitable organization:

1. Write a mission statement. Grab a pen and a notepad, a delicious cup of cappuccino, and write a mission statement that answers the following questions:

- What will your charity be called?

- Who will it serve?

- What is its purpose?

Once you have a written this statement, write down what you intend to accomplish one month, one year, and five years from today. Finally, what is the ultimate goal for your charity? It is important to visualize the future of your organization for you to recognize what it can, and will, achieve. For me, it is to feed *all* of the impoverished kids in America.

2. Promote your charity. At these early stages, you may need to serve as your own spokesperson, or you can ask someone to volunteer to do this for you. If you are going to speak on behalf of your charity, I recommend that you select one individual who can serve as your back-up spokesperson in case you are unable to attend an engagement. My nephew, Sylvano, is the Vice President of Caterina's Club, and he speaks at events in my absence. It behooves you to coordinate and attend as many occasions as possible to get the word out about your program. Now that you have a mission statement, it will be easier to share this vision with others.

There are many different avenues you can explore when it comes to promoting your charity. Contact local newspapers and radio stations. Set up social media pages such Facebook, Twitter, and Instagram to post news and pictures about your progress. Network with other organizations, requesting that you speak briefly at their events. It's worth the investment to find a competent and experienced publicist. I personally credit my publicist for all the media attention that Caterina received. Now is the time to get in the public eye to make sure that as many people know about your philanthropic pursuits as possible.

3. Apply for a 501(c)(3). A 501(c)(3) permits you to be officially recognized as a charity and will also allow your organization to be tax-exempt. This occurs with the understanding that you will not personally profit from your charity. Once you apply for a 501(c)(3), it may take two to three years for your application to be processed and approved.

4. Select a fiscal sponsor. Since you may be waiting for some time to officially become a charity, I recommend that you carefully choose a fiscal sponsor. A fiscal sponsor has a 501(c)(3) itself, and it also sponsors others organizations that may not yet have the means or the approval to run their charity independently. For a fee, your fiscal sponsor will serve as the middleman, so to speak, between your organization and the IRS. They are equipped to handle your finances and assist you in legal matters. Good fiscal sponsors provide financial advice, will most likely manage several charities, and will encourage your organization's independence. That is, if you haven't yet applied for a 501(c)(3) by the time you obtain a fiscal sponsor, they will advise you to do so. An additional word about fiscal sponsors: even when your application does go through, I recommend that you stick with your fiscal sponsor a few months longer than necessary. I know you will excited about being officially recognized as a charitable organization, but there is a lot of work that comes with that title, and you will want to ask your fiscal sponsor as many questions as possible to make sure all of your ducks are in a row.

5. Begin your search for a lawyer and CPA, or Certified Public Accountant. Now that you are on your own, you will need to be on top of your own legal matters and bookkeeping. Just as you may have worked with one or two fiscal sponsors before you identified the one that best met your needs, you may not wish to settle with the first lawyer or CPA that comes your way. An ideal CPA is one who has experience with charitable organizations. If you have a business of your own, such as I do, the bookkeeper you have already may or may not be capable of handling your charity's finances. Because the IRS has much stricter rules and regulations for charities, it is crucial that you select a CPA who has experience in this area.

6. Choose members who wish to be elected for your Executive Board. One of the legal requirements for a charity is to have an Executive Board. Your Executive Board will meet regularly, and, adhering to the by-laws it has established, will vote for issues pertaining to your organization. The Executive Board will determine where your money will be spent; in our case at Caterina's Club, I decided that if any expense is greater than $5,000, the Board must approve it. When searching for members to serve on your Executive Board, I recommend that you seek out one or two people who know you and your philanthropic interests well. It breaks my heart when I hear about individuals who are kicked out of the charity they began themselves!

7. Select your Advisory Board. The Advisory Board will not vote on any issues. They will provide you with valuable advice and will also work to promote your charity. Choose members who are respected leaders in the community, who have a great interest in the work you do, and who can reach out to various subgroups. As a restaurateur, not every member of my community knows me. However, by having individuals on my Advisory Board who are doctors or CEO's or professional athletes, I am given access to different types of people who may want to support Caterina's Club.

Napoleon Hill once said, "Strength and growth come only through continuous effort and struggle." It will not be easy to start a charity. Even today, I continue to work hard to see Caterina's Club reach its full potential. Many people believe that since I've been on CNN, I must be rich. But just like anyone else, I work very hard to pay my mortgage each month. It is my hope that my personal journey will serve as an inspiration to others.

If you have the heart and the passion, you will see that you can overcome any obstacle before you. For me, just to see the kids smile makes it all worth it. You will soon learn for yourself that with your success comes the success of so many others. And so, as you take the first step to seeing your charity become a reality, I leave you with a few final pieces of wisdom I've learned along the way:

- never give up
- respect your friends
- always listen
- ask for help when you need it
- never forget where you came from
- take time to talk to others
- do something about your passion
- thank people every day

. . . And of course, love your Mamma. Ciao!

About Bruno

Bruno Serato, Restaurateur/Proprietor

It's the quintessential American success story. A young man immigrates to the United States with nothing more than a dream and $200 in his pocket, works hard and creates one of the culinary world's most respected and lauded fine dining establishments –the Anaheim White House – with Presidents, royalty and A-list celebrities among his loyal guests. However, it's his charity work that has fueled his international celebrity.

In homage to his own humble beginnings, Serato has made it a priority to give back to those less fortunate in the community. In honor of his mother, he founded Caterina's Club in 2005, an organization dedicated to making sure the region's most vulnerable population – its children – receive a hot meal before they are tucked into bed each evening. Seven nights a week he prepares dinner that is transported to 1,000 "motel kids," thus named because their poverty-stricken parents are unable to afford more permanent housing. In addition, he has begun placing some of these families into homes by helping them overcome the major stumbling block – coming up with the security deposit and first and last month's rent.

Serato's extreme generosity has earned him worldwide status. He was named one of CNN's 10 Heroes of the Year and has been featured in magazines (*People, Elle, Vogue, Riviera*), television (*CBS Evening News, CNN, Univision*) and newspapers (*New York Times, Los Angeles Times, OC Register*) countless times. He was honored on the steps of the U.S. Capitol with a humanitarian award, given a star on the Anaheim Walk of Stars, and received any number of proclamations, Man of the Year awards and other forms of recognition. Perhaps his highest honor was being knighted by the Italian Government, thus earning him the title, Sir Bruno Serato.

Today, he continues to run his highly successful Italian steakhouse and extends his generosity to many other nonprofits besides Caterina's Club. He even earned national attention when he donated formal dinners accommodating 100 guests to 200 different nonprofits. While his prowess in the kitchen knows no bounds, so too does his generosity.

CHAPTER 4

MASTERMIND GROUP – WHEN 1 + 1 DOES NOT EQUAL 2

BY ARTHUR MAGOULIANITI

There is a powerful success strategy that has been used by successful individuals since as far back as 500 BC, which delivers extraordinary results and much more than the sum of the parts. In fact, the results that can be obtained by applying this strategy can be so extraordinary, they can seem downright spooky, magical even.

The strategy has been used by people such as Socrates and Gandhi. It has been used by some of the greatest tycoons in history, such as the steel magnate Andrew Carnegie, the legendary author Napoleon Hill, the famous inventor Thomas Edison, Industrialist Henry Ford and politician, and the scientist and inventor Ben Franklin, to name but a few of the famous ones. And today, it is still in use and becoming even more popular by those that recognize its value and how much it has to offer.

Even though it is not a new idea by any account, most people are still oblivious to what this strategy is and how potent it can be in transforming their personal and professional lives. Thanks to Hill who, in 1937, wrote the classic bestselling book, *Think and Grow Rich*, many more people have come to know about, and make use of this tool, which Hill called The Driving Force and his 9th step to riches.

Based on his interviews of 500 of the most successful people at that time, Hill distilled the practices that were common across these individuals to come up with the content of his book – which includes this strategy, the one he called the Mastermind principle or Masterminding.

In this book Hill said, "Analyze the record of any man who has accumulated a great fortune, and many of those who have accumulated modest fortunes, and you will find that they have either consciously or unconsciously employed the mastermind principle."

He continued, "No individual may have great power without availing himself of the 'Master Mind'. This form of cooperative alliance has been the basis of nearly every great fortune. Your understanding of this great truth may definitely determine your financial status."

Now although Hill refers to great fortunes, this principle is not only limited to generating great wealth, but is also applicable to all other goals and objectives that people may have.

He goes on further to define the mastermind principle as the "Coordination of knowledge and effort, in a spirit of harmony, between two or more people, for the attainment of a definite purpose."

In other words, a mastermind is when two or more people come together to form an alliance of minds, to share their ideas, skills and experience to help each other move forward towards a common goal or individual goals – by creating innovative solutions to life, business challenges and obstacles.

It is important to note that Masterminding is not just another meeting or a networking opportunity in the normal sense. Masterminding is an alliance, a close team of individuals who are committed to either working on making a single goal a reality or helping each other to make their individual goals a reality.

Masterminding is akin to having your very own team who will support and challenge you simultaneously to achieve what you want. Typically a Mastermind Group will have individuals from different walks of life and industries who have distinctly different sets of experiences, and from this depth and breadth of knowledge – amazingly creative ideas, solutions and action plans can be and are derived.

What makes the Masterminding process magical though is that when you bring people together in a spirit of harmony and single focus, ideas come to you out of this collaboration that you would never have thought of yourself. It is as if you have tapped into a whole new stream of intelligence. Hill refers to this in his book, "No two minds ever come together without, thereby, creating a third, invisible, intangible force which may be likened to a third mind." Our brains simply work better in collaboration – that is just how we are wired.

You could describe it by using the metaphor of people building a human bridge to reach the fruit on a branch that is just out of sight and out of reach. On their own they could not have achieved it, but working together not only can they now see the fruit, but they can actually devise a way to get hold of it.

Mastermind groups can be created for just about anything—from a group for entrepreneurs, to a group of industry specialists, to a group of parents and even a group for children. The concept is available to all and all can benefit from it and there are a great many benefits to be gained.

THE MANY BENEFITS OF A MASTERMIND GROUP

Masterminding is a win/win for all. All members of the mastermind are supported, and in turn, support others in the group. In a properly run group, each person gets a turn to ask for help, contacts, advice and tap into the experience of others and everyone gains both individually and from the group experience.

Another benefit is that you end up creating amazing friendships and social relationships that can turn into profitable business partnerships as you have already established trust and have got to know the different participants, how they think, act and work.

Within this supportive environment, you are encouraged to grow and try out new ideas and take actions which you may not have previously done on your own. This can lead to the opening up of whole new areas in your life and business, as well as leading to an increase in confidence in yourself and your abilities that you might have lacked before.

Within a group with varied experience and knowledge, you can tap into the skills and experience of others, brainstorm new ideas and magnify what is possible for you and have many more options available to you than you might have had on your own.

When you marry this confidence with the innovative and creative ideas that the group comes up with, to solve problems and challenges, you can design a robust action plan which you can trust and achieve amazing results for yourself.

Masterminding also provides a great platform for accountability, and we all need more accountability in our lives, to get the stuff important stuff done – the stuff that we said we would get done. The important tasks in our lives are easy to do and easy not to. With the right support structure and accountability we are more likely to do them (by 90% it is reported), and hence ultimately are more likely to see the results we want to see.

HOW TO FORM AND RUN A SUCCESSFUL MASTERMIND GROUP

Before you go about creating a group and inviting people into that group, it is useful to first get clear on what you would like the group to achieve or focus on as you can then invite the people that are most relevant to that purpose in terms of experience and knowledge. Without a strong motive and direction, it will be very easy for the group to slide backwards and become more of a social event and an opportunity to catch up and chat instead of a highly-functioning and productive team.

Who you invite into your group is the next critical factor to its success. Because this is not a social gathering, you don't want to invite people based purely on the merits that you like them and that you get on well with them. Unless you are creating a personal alliance this won't help you move forward much in terms of your focus—whether it be career, job role or financially-oriented.

The type of people to consider are people who are already in a place where you would like to ultimately get to, or at least they may be a little more advanced on the path you are heading. You may think why would people more advanced than I am join such a group. In fact, most people are not in a mastermind group and would happily join one if they don't have to arrange it. They'll be happy to meet the various people in your group to build their networks and improve their results.

Chemistry is another important factor in the selection of the participants. You really only want members that you connect with and who can work well in a team. Now, that doesn't mean you only want people that won't challenge you – that won't help you grow – but you want to ensure that you don't bring anyone aboard that is naturally argumentative or combative. Also, don't have anyone that is so closed off or shy that they won't contribute to the group. Align yourself with people who have similar values as yourself and who want to grow, both in their personal and business lives.

One way to ensure that you select the right people for you and the group is to start with one person at a time on a trial basis for a month or two, see how that goes, then bring on a third for a trial period as well, and, if it works, ask them to stay. If not, terminate the arrangement. Keep going until you have a full team. The participants also all need to be highly motivated individuals who are willing to serve others as well as ask for support when required.

Even with the above screening process, you might still find some people who don't keep to their commitment of regular attendance or who give rise to integrity and trust issues that come up. Be prepared to deal with these head on and ask offenders to leave, otherwise they will contaminate the whole group and bring everyone's energy down, which is exactly the opposite of what you want to achieve.

Confidentiality is key and needs to be agreed on from the outset. In order for people to participate fully and openly, it is imperative that participants feel safe to open up without risking the chance that what they say will find itself outside of the group and in the public domain. Signing a confidentiality agreement prior to joining the group is certainly a possibility and a recommendation to help emphasize this critical requirement.

In order to maintain the integrity of the Mastermind Group, you ideally want a group size of about seven people, with a minimum of five. Anything bigger and meetings will take longer and not everyone will get a chance to be heard. Anything smaller and you will lose the flow and dynamism of the group as there are bound to be occasional absences.

A Mastermind group can meet face-to-face, via phone or even online with the recent developments of technology such as Google Hangouts and Skype. Meetings can be scheduled weekly, bi-weekly or monthly, depending on the schedules of the participants. However, monthly meetings, supported by emails in-between meetings as required, seem to work really well as it allows for time to take action on the items discussed in the meetings.

It is critical for the success of a Mastermind Group that a commitment is made by all participants to prioritise and attend each meeting to maintain the flow and get the most out of each meeting.

The group needs to have a leader to hold the focus of the group, to ensure smooth operation and to encourage those that might not normally talk too much and help silence those that do! This leadership role can be rotated or it can be held permanently by just one person, typically that would be the person that started the group.

It also helps to have an agenda for each meeting as well as a timekeeper as timing is critical – to start and end on time while ensuring that every person has had a chance to speak and be heard. With this in mind, it helps to rotate the first speaker for each meeting – so that a different person begins the meeting each time for variety as well as equality of timing and focus.

The best way to actually get going with a Mastermind Mind group is either to just go ahead and start one and learn as you go along, or you can search online for any number of virtual and local Mastermind Groups offered by various organisations. Whichever way you choose to go, ensure that you make getting into a Mastermind Group a priority. Short of getting a personal coach, it is probably the next quickest way to transform your business and your life with exponential progress.

About Arthur

Arthur Magoulianiti, CHPC is a High Performance Coach, Author and Entrepreneur. His driving principle is that we all deserve to have a life that we love, not just live in, and the best way to do that is through creating it. It's not always our first career or even our second that will give us what we strive for. Arthur knows this firsthand. His initial career focus was Electrical Engineering but he felt there was something better out there for him, something that aligned with his entrepreneurial spirit and passion for strengthening the communities he lived in. Through his journey he found a natural fit in private coaching for entrepreneurs and business leaders. He helps people take the "Now what?" out of their equations, and brings them to the point where they can implement the ideas that will transition them to their greater potential.

Gaining recognition as a Certified High Performance Coach with The Burchard Group, and as a certified coach, trainer, and speaker with The John Maxwell Leadership Team, Arthur is a craftsman of his trade. He has experienced many things in his own life journey where he knew what he wanted, and could even envision it, but it was not happening. He became wholly committed to finding ways to help others avoid that same frustration, and as a result he is an empathetic, action-driven coach. Change isn't easy and Arthur helps make it more manageable through guiding people on how to adjust their mindset – so they can open up the doors to the personal and professional success they desire. Today, Arthur works in the United States and United Kingdom helping individuals achieve exponential shifts in their productivity, psychology, physiology, persuasion, presence, and purpose.

One of the distinctions that lends to Arthur's success at what he does is his approach to helping his clients. He is rooted in the belief that a coach is a mirror that can show clients how they are holding themselves back. Most people do have the answers, but lack the belief in themselves to pursue what matters most to them; what will give them financial freedom and emotional freedom. Arthur not only helps people in that rut believe, he also inspires them to act, and it works!

Arthur is a firm believer that when you contribute to people's lives and help them create a life they love that it will trickle outward. It doesn't start with changing the world; it is about helping change one person's life for the better so they can live a life they love in a powerful, meaningful way.

When Arthur isn't helping his clients conquer the obstacles that are hindering them from reaching their mind's summit, he enjoys living the island life on Cyprus with his wife and two children. In order to keep achieving his personal best he enjoys challenging himself with activities that push his previous personal bests, including ultra marathons, climbing Mt. Kilimanjaro, practicing Krav Maga and taking advantage of all the outdoor activities that exist in this world.

Email: info@arthurmagoulianiti.com
Website: www.arthurmagoulianiti.com
Contact (954) 416-3394

CHAPTER 5

SECRETS TO BOOMING SUCCESS IN BUSINESS AND LIFE

BY CHRISTINA SKYTT

To make a change in the world we have to start with ourselves. Living in sync with who you really are liberates you to experience your most optimal life. When you stay in tune with who you really are, your creativity comes alive. When you try to be somebody else, you get out of sync, off beat, and thrown off course. Being authentic is in my view the most important ingredient in today's busy environment. Learn to be comfortable with who you truly are. Embrace the value of your own unique brand, and do so unapologetically. Never be afraid to be the real you. Like the saying goes, "You were born an original; don't die a copy."

Be yourself - everybody else is already taken.
~ Oscar Wilde

I know from working with clients in executive level positions that their most daring goals are possible to achieve once they had defined them as, what I call Power Goals. My passion is to see people grow and I want people from all walks of life to experience that same excitement and level of success.

For the longest time I wanted to reach broader audiences in new and exciting ways, but I didn't dare to put it into words. Once I clarified and defined my Power Goals, and acknowledged my true desires, my enthusiasm was full on. My Power Goal was to write a book, write it in English (even though my first language is Swedish), get it published in the United States (despite the fact that I had no contacts in the publishing industry) and I wanted my book to become a bestseller. Honestly, this was a Power Goal so big and so scary I didn't even believe it myself. But that is really what a Power Goal is all about - to define a goal so big you have never come close to it before, a goal so scary you have no idea how to reach it, but a goal you desire so much that you're willing to do anything to reach it. I started working on achieving my Power Goal and my book did become a #1 International Bestseller, was published in the U.S., and with an amazing Foreword by Bob Proctor.

I want to share with you my special tips on how to create positive shifts in your life, for your booming success in health, wealth and lifestyle.

1. WHAT IS IT THAT YOU REALLY WANT?

Most people don't have a clear direction in life, let alone "why" they live the life they're living or what they really want to achieve.

Most of us have never allowed ourselves to want what we truly want, because we can't see how it's going to manifest. Saying "I have to" has no inspiration in it, but "I want" is a strong force. If you are not clear on what you want, then you can never get what you want. It's like ordering soup in a restaurant, even though you want chicken. Then, when you get the soup, you end up feeling disappointed by the waiter bringing you the "wrong" dish.

Are you living the life you want to live? Or do you feel a desire for more? Do you feel discontent with where you are, but you're not clear on what you'd love to create . . . so you feel stagnant?

Your "why" is what gives you purpose in life, creates energy and makes you want to jump out of bed on a Monday morning.

It's extremely important to create clarity about your true "why". Tune in to your passion. Get clear on what you want. Set clearly written goals of what you want to accomplish. Be very specific, stating for each goal how much and by when you will accomplish it. This way, you make your goals measurable. You also need to keep your goals in front of you, write them down, say them out loud every day. Then believe that you will receive. Allow it to start happening.

As we grow, so do our goals. In order to be successful in accomplishing your authentic life goals and dreams, you need to be in alignment with your "why" and know exactly what you want.

2. PRACTICE POSITIVITY

To receive what you want you must feel good about YOU. Think about all the perfect things about you. As you think perfect thoughts, as you feel good about yourself, you are on the frequency of your perfect self.

If you decide to be the positive you, with no more moaning, complaining or grumbling, good things revolve and happen. The interesting fact is that when you answer in a positive way, even if you don't feel it, you will undoubtedly make yourself and everyone around you more upbeat. It really works.

You cannot help the world by focusing on the negative things. Instead of focusing on problems, give your attention and energy to trust, love, abundance, education, and peace. There will be more and your positivity scale will go up.

Laughter attracts joy, releases negativity, and leads to miraculous cures. Think of how you feel when you have a deep, hearty, belly laugh. Isn't it wonderful to belly laugh, and if it's catchy, those around will smile or laugh when you do.

People who accomplish great things are aware of the
negative, but give all of their mental energy to the positive.
~ Bob Proctor

To make a relationship work, focus on what you appreciate about the other person, and not your complaints about your spouse. When you focus on the positive, you will get more of it in return.

Being playful by injecting some humor helps us keep perspective when life gets tricky. As Albert Einstein said, "Play is the highest form of research." If we take work too seriously we will never do anything new. To set yourself and your work apart from the rest there needs to be creativity, energy, commitment, excitement and humor. We may be in a serious business, but we don't have to take everything so seriously.

Summary on how to Stay Positive:

- Focus on past successes, instead of letting your inner voice talk about your failures.
- Use your positive energy towards your own development and success, rather than wasting energy on emotions that pull you down.
- Ask yourself what you can do today to really draw the best out of yourself.
- Only use positive words.
- Create a victory log – a written record of your successes.
- Feed your brain with positive messages.
- Use secret mood shifters, such as pleasant memories, nature, your favorite music, your dog, your kids, etc. They can change your feelings and shift your frequency in an instant.
- Be open and enthusiastic about the constant changes that occur in life.
- Find opportunities in every difficulty and remember "there are no mistakes, only opportunities from which we learn."

3. VISUALIZATION

Visualization is the process of creating pictures in your mind of yourself enjoying what you want, your goal. The reason visualization is so powerful is because as you create pictures in your mind of seeing yourself as your future self, you are generating thoughts and feelings of having it now.

Decide what you want. Believe you can have it. Believe you deserve it and it's possible for you. Then close your eyes every day for a few minutes and visualize having what you want, feeling the feelings of already having it. It's this feeling that really creates the attraction and it then becomes your experience. Be grateful that it's already there for you.

4. HANG AROUND THE RIGHT PEOPLE

We become like the people we hang out with. If you want to be more successful, you have to start hanging out with more successful people. It's like playing tennis with somebody that plays better than you. It will challenge you to improve your tennis. If you play with people that are not as good as you, they will improve their tennis but you will not. Growing and nurturing healthy relationships is not an option but a necessity for achieving success.

When "like-minded" and "like-spirited" people get around each other, they ignite each other's creative energy. You know that incredible feeling you get when you're around someone who "gets" you? You feel like you're on the same page, speaking the same language, and humming the same tune. Things seem to click almost effortlessly. Feeling understood, genuinely accepted, and valued allows you to feel emotionally safe, which liberates you to be more open, receptive, and genuinely expressive. Find "like-minded" people – to stay on the same agenda as you and get you inspired. They don't necessarily have to agree with you, but you will benefit from their creative criticism.

It's time to start looking at who you hang around and figure out if the people you surround yourself with are supportive of what you are trying to achieve. Being in a community that believes in you is critical.

It is "super" important to be surrounded with those who have a positive attitude, a solution-oriented approach to life – people who know that they can accomplish whatever they set out to do.

Get a community of positive people, so called cheerleaders, and strive for WIN-WIN relationships. Understand that a "win" for all is ultimately a better long-term solution for everyone and for you personally. Genuinely strive for mutually-beneficial solutions or agreements in your relationships.

5. LOVE

There is no greater power than the power of love. Love is not spoken about in business, yet it's a potential super power. During my executive coaching career, I've experienced that with a lot of the top executives their weak point was not the performance at work, but the fact that they have lost the love for their work, their colleagues, friends, families and ultimately for themselves.

The feeling of love is the highest frequency in life and I'm convinced you cannot excel without love. If you can feel love for what you work with, the people you work with, the friends you have and your family, you will release enormous energy and excel at whatever you focus on. If you can wrap every thought in love, if you could love everything and everyone, your life would be transformed.

Treat yourself with love and respect and you will attract people who show you love and respect. It becomes a positivity loop.

I am sure that when I look back at my life I won't be moved by the amount of work I've done or how much money I've made, but I will be moved by the lives that I've touched and those that have touched me.

Imagine if we could feel excitement, joy,
gratitude and love every day.
When you celebrate the good feelings,
you'll draw to you more good feelings,
and things that make you feel good.
~ Lisa Nichols

6. ACTION IS THE KEY TO SUCCESS

Achieving any big goal is achieving a series of small goals. The best way to eat an elephant is one bite at a time. Once you have decided on reaching your big dream you will have to break it down into smaller goals and then break it down to your weekly and daily activities.

So many people have great ideas, but most of them are not acted upon. To achieve the next level of success, you must take consistent and massive action. It's really about transforming great ideas into reality.

The secret of getting ahead is getting started.
The secret of getting started is breaking your complex,
overwhelming tasks into small,
manageable tasks and then starting on the first one.
~ Mark Twain

You cannot make somebody else do your push-ups, your exercise, meditations, studying, learning a new language, practicing new skills or running a marathon. You have to do it yourself, to get any value from it.

Stop talking about what you should do and start doing it! It is time to stop waiting for: perfection, inspiration, permission, reassurance, someone to change, the right people to come along, the kids to leave home, a clear set of instructions or a new job.

There will never be a perfect time to start, so just start! And remember, the last letters in satisfaction are action. Action leads to satisfaction!

7. CUT THE EXCUSES FOR NOT GETTING STARTED

So many people allow themselves to have excuses for not getting started.

- If I only had money…
- If I only had more time…
- If the economy was different…
- If I were only younger…
- If I wasn't always sick…
- If I had only been given a chance…
- If I had a good education…
- If I did not have to work so hard…
- If I only had somebody to help me…
- If I could only meet "the right people"…

… or

- I'm too tired.
- I'm too busy.
- I forgot.
- I can't afford it.

Examine yourself carefully if you hide behind any of these excuses. If you do, it's now time to stop. You will never achieve your dream if you allow yourself to be a victim and feel sorry for yourself. Don't position yourself as a victim. It's crucial to take full responsibility for your own life.

If you have the courage to see yourself as you really are and the alibis you provide for yourself, you have the possibility to correct and learn from the experience.

8. EXPECT TURBULENCE

When you start to challenge yourself and change, you can be sure that both internal and external turbulence will begin and there will be setbacks. If you are aware of this, it will make it easier for you to handle.

When you try something new, you will feel awkward and uncomfortable. That's because you're moving out of your comfort zone, where you feel comfortable, secure and at home. Personal development always happens outside of your comfort zone.

If everything is easy and harmonious, we learn nothing. When things seem to be tough, those are the biggest lessons and ultimately we grow and learn from everything. Be brave. Harvest the good.

> *When anything 'bad' happens, I remember that everything*
> *that ever happens to me has within it the seeds*
> *of something better. I look for the upside*
> *rather than the downside. I ask myself,*
> *"Where is the greater benefit in this event?"*
> ~ Jack Canfield

9. GRATITUDE

Gratitude is the most powerful process for shifting your energy and bringing more of what you want into your life. Gratitude is the single most important ingredient to changing things for the better and living a successful life.

Many people focus on the one thing they want and forget to be grateful for all the things they already have. If you are grateful for what you already have, you will attract more good things into your life.

Being grateful is a choice. It's about learning from challenging situations and taking the good out of it. Look for the gift in everything and be grateful here and now. Even if you focus on your ultimate goal, make sure to appreciate the positive things that happen along the way. Starting each day with writing a list of what you're grateful for, will set the tone for the day. Start by writing down: I am so happy and grateful for... and then fill it out. Take action and do this.

As Oprah Winfrey said:
Be grateful for what you have and you'll end up having more. If you concentrate on what you don't have you will never have enough.

In conclusion, if you are looking to create positive shifts in your life, embrace my special tips for booming success in health, wealth and lifestyle. I know that if you take to heart these powerful lessons in personal growth, then BOOM, you'll see amazing things happening in your own life.

About Christina

Christina Skytt is a #1 International Bestselling Author, inspirational speaker and founder of the Power Goals Academy. She has worked for twenty years in international business and more than ten years as a top executive coach.

Christina has developed a specific methodology and results-oriented activities to help people take on greater challenges and produce breakthrough results. Her proven formula for success reached global acclaim with her international bestseller, *Power Goals™: 9 Clear Steps to Achieving Life-Changing Goals.*

Her book contains proven principles for success used by top achievers from all walks of life. Christina guides her clients though the nine-step process that includes mapping out the starting-point, setting powerful goals, creating a vision, addressing your pre-programming, assembling a supportive team, taking action, maintaining a positive attitude, handling turbulent situations, and not forgetting to celebrate the achievement of your Power Goals.

As a speaker, Christina has conducted keynote speeches, workshops and seminars and has made many presentations on topics such as Success Principles, Power Goals, Positive habits, behaviors and choices as well as on International Marketing.

Christina is a graduate of Stockholm School of Economics and Business Administration with a Master's degree in International Business and Marketing. She is one of the earliest champions of top-level coaching worldwide.

Christina is recognized as a top trainer for her unique approach to serving her clients. She has been personally mentored by Bob Proctor, Jack Canfield, Mark-Victor Hansen, and Peggy McColl, to be the next generation leader in personal development.

You can connect with Christina at:
Christina@powergoalsacademy.com
www.facebook.com/Powergoalsacademy

For additional details on Christina:
Please call +46 (709)66 44 60 (direct)

CHAPTER 6

REWEAVING THE FABRIC OF LIFE AFTER LOSS

BY DONNA FARRIS

INTRODUCTION

For over 20 years, my career has led me to work with many people going through major life transitions due to loss. I have worked as a grief counselor with both individuals and groups helping people recover after the death of a loved one. As a hospice social worker, I walked through the journey of the last stage of life with patients and families. Although I had personally experienced loss, none of my close loved ones had passed away. Yes, I had been through the challenge of a divorce after a 30-year marriage, which is the death of a relationship. However, my divorce had been a personal decision within my control. Despite many unexpected emotional and financial challenges accompanying a divorce, it had been a choice. With that experience, I learned a great deal about how to be resilient. It took me time to grieve that loss and recover with the help of the information that I share with you in this chapter..

In the winter of 2012 came the news that rocked my world: my seeming healthy boyfriend of just two years, Doug, was diagnosed with Stage IV colon cancer. With oncology social work as my specialty for many years, I was not allowed the luxury of denial. I knew how serious his condition was, although his oncologist had informed me privately that if all went right, he could live 7 or 8 years. Unfortunately, nothing went "right!" Doug was wise and kind enough to give me the opportunity to back out of our relationship. I never once gave any thought to just walking away. I had seen the emotional devastation of patients left behind after a cancer diagnosis. I could not be "that girl" who abandoned a loved one in need. He needed me and I thought, "I can do this."

Doug's cancer journey was a long story of multiple surgeries, emergency hospitalizations, chemotherapy, radiation, and ultimately significant pain and suffering. No matter how much I thought I knew or how much experience I had, nothing prepared me for what we went through; the indignities, the callous treatment by some medical professionals, and constant stress of the unknown. After a very courageous battle, he passed away two years later.

I was very lucky to have the support of a very knowledgeable team of hospice nurses during the journey. However, when he died, I quite honestly felt like I had been through a war. I was exhausted and depleted in every way possible. During the two years I helped him with his treatment, I had been able to keep all the balls in the air; working full time for hospice, leading a weekly bereavement support group for a local hospital, facilitating two annual retreats for 100 cancer survivors, and maintaining a private practice. After Doug passed away, people kept saying to me "Write a book." Were they nuts! I was exhausted.

So, fast forward a few years and then, out of the blue, I received an opportunity to write a chapter in this great book, *Boom*. It got me thinking about what I had learned along the journey that unfortunately did not end in Doug's healing but left me with the need to heal. What strategies could I offer others for enhancing their health, wealth, or lifestyle when they may be as depleted and exhausted as I was? What helped *me* to move on to a brighter future? I decided to take this opportunity to share some strategies that helped me and many others I had worked with over the years.

All of us will experience major losses in our lifetimes. Most likely, these losses will affect us emotionally, socially, and financially. Whatever the loss, giving yourself the opportunity to heal and move on are essential to finding a new and happy life - your personal "Boom".

The following pages offer some guidelines to help you through your personal healing journey. The overarching goal is to not "get stuck". I have seen many people stalled on their journey to recovery; stalled in anger, fear, and depression. You can compensate for personal losses; like finding a rewarding career after losing a dream job, finding happiness again after losing a loved one, and still enjoying life although facing a serious health challenge. In other words, avoiding getting stuck will make you stronger and more resilient.

There are no timelines for how long it will take to feel a sense of recovery. Loss recovery time is very personal. It is related to the impact of the loss on you in all areas of your life. I just encourage you to start wherever you are at this time, and realize that this is a yet another journey – take that first step.

THE THREE "R'S" OF LOSS RECOVERY

I. REALIZATION

The Realization stage generally lasts for a few weeks to a few months for some people.

1. *Accept the reality of your loss.*
   In this time of early loss, shock, denial, and disbelief are normal. If a loved one has been ill for a length of time, their death can still be a shock. Even if you know for sure your spouse is moving out in a divorce, when it finally happens, it is still a shock. It takes time to finally realize no one is "coming back", and you are now alone.

2. *Accept the meaning of your loss.*
   After the death of a loved one, you no longer have the role

of partner, spouse, parent, or child. Now, your role may be single, widow, or widower. Your world has suddenly turned upside down. You may well have lost your most important job, that of caring for the love you love. That can be a major life transition.

3. *Understand the reactions to loss in early grief.*
Typical reactions in this early stage are disbelief and a feeling of being in a fog. You may frequently feel tearful at inopportune times, or may have difficulty concentrating. Short-term memory issues are common. Other possible issues are feelings of anxiety, depressed mood, guilt, and often problems sleeping and eating.

II. REORGANIZATION

Reorganization can sometimes last 1 to 2 years.

1. *Allow yourself time to grieve.*
For many, realizing the need to grieve is difficult. However, a significant loss *must* be acknowledged. Society's message is usually "don't feel bad" or "aren't you over it yet?" It was even hard for me to acknowledge my need to grieve. I could intellectualize about my loss, of course, using what I had learned all those years working in the field. But, now, I had to actually feel the pain. It took me much longer than I thought. I learned I had to be patient with myself and give myself much more tolerance and understanding than I ever did before.

2. *Educate yourself about your loss.*
Learn from the experience of others. Reading books written by others who have gone through similar losses can be very helpful. The Internet has a vast array of resources on any topic; from coping with chronic illness, to job loss, to divorce, or to the death of a loved one. The goal is to educate yourself about grief and loss to help normalize your feelings.

3. *Find a support system.*

From my experience, I am a firm believer in the power of groups to facilitate healing. Support groups are an excellent source of education and resources. Sharing and listening to the feelings of others in similar situations reduces the feeling of isolation and the fear that often accompanies life's losses. Sharing equals healing. Also, be willing to share your real feelings with those friends and relatives who are supportive and understanding of what you are going through.

4. *Seek professional support as needed.*

This may well be the time to find a professional team to help with your new challenges. If you need help with finances, you may need to call on an accountant, a financial planner, or a tax consultant. I must admit that finances were not my strength, but my fears decreased with the help of a financial planner and a tax accountant - neither of which I had felt any need for in the past. You might also need legal advice to help you navigate through changes in your life. For help with emotional impact of loss, I strongly recommend getting individual counseling with a therapist specializing in loss recovery. This is especially important if you suspect that you are feeling stuck emotionally in depression, fear, or anger. The sooner you get help, the sooner your recovery.

5. *Adjust to your new environment.*

You may well be alone at home for the first time in your life, and it can be frightening. For many, it may seem like this is the time when things around the house start to break down. Little things suddenly feel overwhelming. You might have to call on professional help to maintain your home and your property. Having to manage everything alone can be daunting especially when you are not fully functioning because of your grief. It is not a weakness to seek help.

Loneliness can be a major problem. Some people will ask a friend or relative to move in with them as they work through their grief, or they get a pet for company. Use your support team to come up with a personal plan of action to deal with your loneliness.

6. *Nurture yourself.*

For some people, this seems to be the hardest thing to do. Many of us are great at caring for other people, but we neglect ourselves. In a time of grief, loss, or transition, it is more important than ever to take care of ourselves.

I work with my clients to help them to create a holistic health plan focusing on body mind, and spirit. People need to follow up on their medical needs often neglected in dealing with the medical needs of loved ones. Diet and exercise take on greater importance as they seem to be the first things to suffer when we are under stress. Getting adequate sleep and taking time for relaxation and fun are essential for recovery. Meditation and/or prayer are very healing. Reconnecting with a spiritual support system of church or religious activities can be a helpful part of the plan. All of these activities are under our control and essential for regaining our equilibrium after a loss.

III. REWEAVING

Reweaving usually occurs in the second-to-third year after a major loss. If you were able to move through the first two stages (Realization and Reorganization) without getting "stuck", you will find yourself focused on the future.

1. *Assess your priorities*

Acknowledge that you are not the same person you were before the loss. You have developed resilience in the recovery process and you are now transformed by what you have been through. You have increased your compassion for others going through similar circumstances. Your relationships with family and friends has changed now that you are establishing your "new normal". Now is the time to decide what is important to you.

2. *Imagine the new life you want.*

This is the time for dreaming. Acknowledge your strengths. Set new goals. Meet new people. Start new projects. You are now moving on into your future. This is the time for exploration. Leave your comfort zone and try new things. Journaling, putting goals into writing, can be helpful in this process.

3. *Move forward in love.*

Love doesn't die, but people and relationships do. As we move toward healing, we must remember the love and let go of the pain. Our loved one is always with us in memories, but those memories change from ones of the pain suffered to ones of the blessings and gifts left behind.. We cannot move forward if we are always looking in the rear view mirror. Have the courage to remember the lessons of the past and move toward the future with hope and love.

SUMMARY

My goal has been to share with you what I've learned personally and professionally about the journey of grief. Grief is a very personal, solitary journey, but it is made easier when shared with others. Look for help from people who are supportive, who really can listen to you and give you help along the way. Grief is an emotional roller coaster; choose fellow travelers on this journey who can handle the ride.

Grief is something that just doesn't go away on its own. It needs to be processed. It needs to be felt. I would encourage you to take the time to actually feel the pain. So, don't drink it away, don't party it away, and don't date it away. Experience fully the loss and the meaning of that loss in your personal life.

I recommend that you give yourself positive messages like: "I can recover" and "I am getting stronger." You will come out with new strengths, new ideas, and a new direction. You can feel whole again with a new purpose or focus in life. Life can be beautiful again. It just takes time, energy, and hope.

Grief is not a terminal illness. You *can* recover, and you *will* recover – if you work at it. As I stated earlier, there is no timetable. I can't tell you it's going to take a month, a year, or several years. Everyone is different; the *depth* of your loss is different. Your main goal is to not get "stuck" while in the process of grieving. If you do feel stuck at any time, please seek professional help. Surround yourself with a healing team of people and after you recover, pay it forward to the next person who will need you in their time of loss.

The following is a brief list of some of resources that were helpful to me:

<u>Books</u>

The Grief Recovery Handbook by John W. James and Russell Friedman.

You Can Heal Your Heart by Louise Hay and David Kessler.

Driving Solo by Susan Covell Alpert.

Internet

There are a vast array of resources to choose from. GriefNet.org has great information.

O'ConnorMortuary.com has a great section on Grief and Healing. I benefitted from their Daily Email Affirmations during the first year of my loss.

About Donna

Donna Farris, LCSW, has been a licensed mental health professional in private practice in Southern California since 1990. Additionally, she has over 25 years of experience as a medical social worker working in acute care hospitals, home care, and hospice settings. She is an accomplished speaker, author, and educator.

Donna's specialty is in oncology, working on several inpatient oncology units. Donna facilitated hospital-based education and support groups for cancer patients and their families for 15 years. She has led weekly grief support and education programs for the past six years. Donna has been a Certified Grief Recovery Specialist since 2012.

As a co-creator of the Healing Odyssey Retreat Program, Donna facilitated empowerment retreats for women cancer survivors for over 18 years. Through that program, she has helped over 1000 women in their emotional recovery from the stresses of cancer.

Donna is a graduate of Pennsylvania State University majoring in Sociology. She has her Masters in Social Work from the University of Connecticut.

Donna was the recipient of the annual St. Joseph Health System Values in Action award for Service in 2004 for her hospital social work. She received the Soroptimist International Ruby Award for Women Helping Women in 2011 for her commitment to women cancer survivors through the Healing Odyssey program.

Donna's energy, compassion, knowledge, and guidance have helped thousands of people over the years to overcome major life challenges and live their best life yet. Her goal is to help others to create a roadmap from a place of fear to a place of peace and healing.

Donna currently has a successful private counseling and consulting practice in Orange County, California. She is a sought-after educator and motivational speaker in the areas of health and wellness.

You can connect with Donna at:
www.donnafarris.com
www.linked.com/donnafarris

CHAPTER 7

WHEN YOU ALMOST DIE, YOU WAKE UP

BY FAHAD BUCHH

Imagine. You are nine years old. The last thing you remember is the world spinning, going dark, falling. The first thing you hear is a machine beeping, strange clicking sounds. You become aware of something up your nose and that air is coming out of it. As you open your eyes, they slowly focus on the sterile sheen of the hospital room.

When I was 9 years old, I went through a life-changing experience; I almost died due to extreme high fevers. My body temperature was at 105+. My parents, panic-stricken, rushed me to the hospital and they saved my life. The doctors said that I had just survived by a few minutes. I was unaware of all of this. When I woke up the next morning in the hospital, I was surprised. The first words that came out of my mouth were, "Where am I?" It might seem surprising, but somehow my nine-year-old brain registered a deep knowing, "I have been given another chance!" Equally surprising was that my nine-year-old brain immediately understood the enormity of that meaning. Something changed inside me. Something beyond the knowing of an ordinary nine year old. I was extremely grateful for this opportunity. Suddenly, I was ready to face the world; face the world in a very grown up way.

The doctors, worried about another episode, played it safe and put me on medication for the next 3 years. They said that I needed to limit myself from physical activities and sports. After this incident, I struggled in school. My parents, society and everyone else told me I had a lot of time to live. So, I never worried about it. After this incident, I realized that life is short. I thought that I really didn't have much time left. I made a decision that day, a decision I have ever since lived with. I decided to never ever blame the world for my problems. I needed to find a way no matter what happened. This illness created a deep realization within me. I needed to make a difference in the world. After that day, my life completely changed. I began taking risks. I stopped playing it safe. I thought that I didn't have much time; I started looking for new opportunities. I respected every precious minute I was living.

A few weeks after the incident, I was walking in my local mall and I saw that a non-profit organization was giving away free Pokémon badges for a promotion. I quickly ran and grabbed two large packages. I had a great idea. Why don't I sell these badges to kids? Immediately, my old mindset told me, "No, don't do that." But, then the memories of my recent experience reminded me of how short life can be and my new mindset said, "take BIG risks." For a moment, I thought about asking my friends for advice. That would have been a wise decision. But, when I told them what I was thinking, they made fun of me. They thought the idea was stupid, and no one would buy the badges.That got me fired up and excited. I knew there and then, that when you are about to act on a new decision, start a new business, or make a new move; there will be people who laugh and make fun of you. However, I believed in me. I held my experience of near death close to me. I decided to take action.

So, I got on my little bicycle and went up to kids in my school ground. I started presenting my first product. My first heroic approach had little success, it resulted in a new profit of only $30. Not bad for a nine year old kid, right? I wanted to do better.

I decided to change my strategy. Instead of approaching kids, who hardly had any money with them, I went door-to-door selling the badges to parents. This new strategy was a major success. I made $90 dollars on my first night. I sold all of my badges within 4 days and made a profit of $200. I used some of the money I earned, to purchase food to feed a homeless cat. The rest of the money, I donated to feed homeless people in my community. I loved helping others.

It was in that moment that my mission in life was revealed to me. I love to make a difference in the lives of other people around me. My friends thought that I was just lucky. What most people don't know is that I was determined and persistent. I heard more NO than YES. I was told "NO" 150 times before I heard my first "YES!" It looked like instant success, but that was just an illusion. Don't fall for that illusion! I proved all my friends wrong, and learned a great lesson. I was sure that in life that I would come across ridicule again. The trick was not reacting to the gossiping and haters. Instead, I would respond by taking the first step towards what scares me most. Whenever I have to decide between two options, I always pick the one that scares me the most.

Later, at the age of 14, I decided to take on another mighty challenge. The memory of my near-death experience was alive within me. I made a decision to play mens' field hockey and represent my high school. I tried out and successfully made the team. I was extremely delighted and scared. Yikes!! I had never ever played field hockey before. Imagine how you would feel if you had to represent your school playing a sport you never played before?

I was curious and I had a good attitude. I practiced every day for 60 days with a great coach. After hours and hours of hard work, dedication and practice, it was time to prove myself. The big tournament was finally here. I travelled with my team for two hours to get to our destination. I was excited, but to be honest, I was nervous. I played relentlessly. I won the under-15 championship. But, that wasn't enough. I always I wanted to go the extra mile. I knew that I could do more, be more and have more. I courageously went up to my coach and asked him to put me in, on the under-18 team. The pressure was enormous. I just kept telling myself, "The thing that scares me the most, is the one I need to pursue." I could face being ridiculed by my colleagues, if I did not perform well. After all, this was nothing compared to death. I have always kept that near-death experience close to me. The result was that I ended up scoring a goal in the under-18 championship.

The secret formula I used was simple, "I just expected it." I expected myself to score. In life, we don't get anything we just want, but we get anything and everything we expect. My team lost the tournament. As usual, I was not satisfied with just scoring one goal. I wanted to know, "What else could I do?" I wanted to win in a bigger way. So, I decided I would come back next year and win the championship. In every great success story, there is hard work behind the glamorous results. When I made the decision, I had no doubt in my mind that I would accomplish my goal. I put my words into action and I practiced three hours every day for the next year.

There were times I wanted to quit, skip practice and I felt like just taking it easy. But, what kept me going was that I wanted to make my whole school proud by winning the championship. I wanted to inspire new young players to join the team.

Sometimes, life seems complicated. This is due to the fact that we have many options to choose from. Life has its ups and downs. One thing that we can keep in mind is that we always have a choice. *I invite you to take on my challenge, of doing the thing you are most afraid to do.* Twitter #MrEnergizer. The things that we fear the most, challenge us and help us grow into stronger and better human beings. Ask yourself this question, "What activity challenges me the most?" Share your responses on Twitter and Facebook. I could have settled for the one goal I scored in the first game, or for just making $30. But, I didn't.

Instead, I raised my standards, aimed high and worked hard with all my energy and played in the tournament. As a result, I won the championship.

Now, if I were to describe in one word how my win made me feel, I would say it was "motivating." Wins in life are the biggest motivators we have. When in doubt, remember your wins. Simply close your eyes and feel how you felt at that moment. I always focus on my wins, I expect to win, and I do win everytime. I learned a lesson from my past experiences that one should live each day abundantly and make the best of it. Although I am in perfectly good health now, my childhood incident changed my life in a positive way.

Here are the 12 steps I use to stay fully alive, take risks and keep winning:

1. *I take complete responsibility of my life* – I stop all blame games and take 100% responsibility for every result I get. Start now and don't wait for tomorrow. We are the creators of our circumstances.

2. *I see every circumstance as an illusion* – My mental mindset is to see real life as a video game. Once we start seeing every situation with this mindset. There is no fear of rejection or loss in our minds. Have this as a motto: "I care but not so much." This mindset helped me sell and make money. I did not care if I made the sales or not. What mattered most was having fun!!

3. *Scarcity can be a good thing if you use it to your advantage* – Time is valuable, each day is a blessing. You will never get back each day. Take the first step towards your goals every day.

4. *Be the most optimistic person you know* – Don't join the "Not-Bad-club." When I ask most individuals how they are doing? They said "Not Bad." Always reply with enthusiasm and a great attitude. This is very important! My optimistic

attitude rubs off on other people like a great computer software. However, if we choose to be pessimistic, it can be a bad mind-virus.

5. *Be absolutely certain about your goals* – In other words, expect it to happen. Everyone called me lucky when I made 200 dollars. But luck is the effect of your internal thought process.

6. *Have a reason bigger than yourself* – A BIG reason can act as a cushion, when things get tough. Your mission in life should drive you. I've never looked back; my mission keeps driving me up to this day.

7. *Keep the fire alive – Love the process of success and don't fall in love with the illusion of the end results.* Raise your standards and have a desire to be, do and accomplish more. Going door-to-door was a challenge, but I overcame it with an intense hunger to be successful and make an impact on other human beings. I learned that I needed to keep pushing when all the odds are against me.

8. *Find your groove* – What songs hit you the hardest? Every good song has a rhythm to it and life also has a similar rhythm. You just have to discover your own rhythm internally. Simply play your favorite song and notice how you feel? That feeling is your inner rhythm. Every activity you engage in must bring this inner groove to the table. This is how I found my strength, even when all the odds were against me. You can do the same just knowing that every activity has a groove to it. You must align your natural groove with the activity you are doing.

9. *Maintain your excellence* – Once your find your groove, now it's important that you consistently feel this groove each minute of your life. Every minute of my life I play a role of a lead hero in my own movie. I feel like a winner and it helps me conquer every barrier you can imagine.

10. *Let your dialogue serve you* – I speak very highly of myself to myself. It's unbelievable how well I speak of myself to myself. Every human being is having a dialogue with themselves all the time. Ask yourself this question – Is the story I tell myself every day serving me? or is it making me weaker?

11. *Your successes are your foundation, not the end result* – Imagine the tallest tower in the world, Burj Khalifa, on a cloudy day. You can't see the top of the building. When we start our journey from the bottom, its important to remember that when we get to our goals, we must continue our journey and never stop being satisfied with what we have become. If we have become generous as human beings then it's important to build on that success and keep going. Become even more generous, never stop. Most people think small. Are you thinking too small? Aim high and don't apologize for it.

12. *Plan your legacy* – Where will you be 50 years from now. Will you matter? Will you have inspired lives because of the work you did? What will you have done for the next generation? I ask these questions to myself every day. I make all my decisions based on these questions. I only take part in activities that will help me create a meaningful legacy.

You will face challenges in life, Make sure
you work hard and strive;
Live a life of purpose and passion,
Do all that with compassion;
~ Fahad Buchh

About Fahad

Fahad Buchh solves business and focus challenges. His goal is to help his clients become more self-reliant, self-confident and self-aware with his practical real world experience of being a young successful entrepreneur. He is the founder of: www.mr-energizer.com. This is a company which helps entrepreneurs find their inner energy and achieve their goals.

Fahad Buchh has been energizing audiences with inspiring keynote presentations that motivates people to identify and pursue their highest aspirations. Fahad helps his audiences reconnect with their true motivation, their core values and the creativity they need to take their performance to the next level.

You can contact Fahad Buchh at:
General questions or enquiries - Info@fahadbuchh.com
Personal email - fahad@fahadbuchh.com
Facebook - https://www.facebook.com/mrenergizerint
Twitter - https://twitter.com/mrenergizerint
Instagram -http://instagram.com/mrenergizerint

CHAPTER 8

WHAT IS YOUR BEST STRATEGY NOW IN 2015 FOR HEALTH CARE COVERAGE?

BY FRANK SALTZBURG

This is a true story about the birth of my daughter, Nicole. Back in 1978, my wife, Sandie, and I were expecting our first child. Sandie had a normal pregnancy with no major problems going into the end of her second trimester. In fact, we were given the green light by her gynecologist to go on our vacation and fly to Bermuda from Philadelphia.

So, on July 9, 1978, we flew to Bermuda and checked into the beautiful Sonesta Beach Hotel located in Paget, Bermuda, in the early afternoon. That night we had an early dinner and were in bed by 11:00pm. Throughout the night Sandie was restless, felt some pressure in her lower abdomen, and did not have a good night's sleep. So, at 5:00am, I called the gynecologist's answering service and he immediately called me back indicating I find out where the closest hospital was in case we needed to travel there. We both showered, got dressed, and went downstairs for our first breakfast at the hotel.

We started to eat our breakfast when Sandie began to feel queasy, was very uncomfortable, and started feeling intermittent pains about two minutes apart. She had to get up from the table and walked out to the lobby. While in the lobby all of a sudden she felt water trickling down her leg under her casual beach shorts. Realizing what was happening, she tried crouching behind a large standing ashtray in the lobby, trying to avoid any possible stares from the ever-increasing water flow. Her water had broken at 9:30am!

I ran to the nearest phone and called a taxi to meet us at the front entrance. The time was now 9:40am. I pleaded to the driver to please get us to the hospital as my wife was already in labor.

At this point her labor was very intense. Contractions were less than two minutes apart. The hospital was about fifteen minutes from the hotel. We were now improvising the Lamaze method based upon what we had seen on TV. Every time Sandie started to feel a painful contraction coming on, I prompted her to breathe short breaths in unison with me while she was squeezing my hand. The taxi driver was freaking out as Sandie was screaming in pain and he would chime in, "Breathe, lady!! Breathe!"

We finally saw the hospital in view but the front entrance driveway was blocked! Our cab driver quickly improvised and literally drove on the sidewalk to the hospital entrance knowing full well a baby was about to be born—literally any minute! We made it to the hospital in fifteen minutes thanks to our driver.

Nurses were waiting with a wheelchair to take my wife right to the delivery room. The time was now 9:55am. I was filling out forms so I could be with Sandie when our baby was born. Meanwhile the medical staff was prepping Sandie for delivery, barely. I no sooner finished all the forms when a British midwife came out to me at 10:10am and announced we had a new baby girl at only 26 weeks…all of 2 pounds, 2 ounces and 17 inches long! And, born completely natural with no drugs. She was a frank breech birth, meaning she came out butt first with her feet near her head. Her chances of survival, at best, were 10%.

I am sharing this story with you as this was a totally unexpected Major Medical event with numerous complications and challenges to experience over the next three months. Our daughter, Nicole (Nikki), was in Childrens' Hospital of Philadelphia for three months, including two and one-half months in neo-natal intensive care. Upon discharge, her total medical bill in 1978 was almost $67,000.

Adjusted for inflation in 2015's terms and the increase in health care costs since 1978, this $67,000 bill would equate to approximately $376,000 today! Who can afford this today and how can you protect yourself from this kind of financial exposure and debt?

The big question is: what is the **best way to minimize your financial exposure INCLUDING minimizing your out-of-pocket expenses** should you have a major catastrophic illness, accident, or unexpected medical event such as what my wife and I experienced?

The most effective way to secure your personal health care coverage goals for you and your family is to simply take advantage of the powerful **Triangle Effect Strategy.**

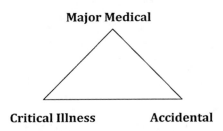

Let's take a closer look at this strategy and how it truly benefits you and your family. At the top of your triangle is what you have known as "Major Medical Coverage", the biggest building block of your health care coverage package. This typically is going to be your hospitalization expenses, surgeries, anesthesia, diagnostic testing, labs, doctor visits, and wellness exams.

However, almost everyone's **Biggest Fear** is how am I going to pay for my deductible and out-of-pocket expenses?

That $2,000, $3,500, or $6,500 deductible appears to be a huge challenge for many. Understandable! The way to tidy this up and still give you a lower premium (monthly payment) is to keep your deductible a bit higher than you may have been accustomed to and **seal off one of your deductible, vulnerable spots** by having **Accidental Coverage** built into your plan.

So, if you or anybody in your family has any type of accident, the accidental portion kicks in first. Having the **accident supplement built into your policy package will pay up to your deductible amount and cover your out-of-pocket expenses, too.**

What does this really do for you?

1. It **eliminates that fear of not having the money** to pay for your deductible and out-of-pocket expenses if you or anyone in your covered family ever experiences an accident.

2. It also **gives you and your family a more comprehensive plan** because now you don't have to worry about a huge outlay of money from your personal savings should there be any accidents.

The reason the accidental coverage is built into your plan as a strategy is because up to 85% of the time when you or a family member ends up in the hospital, it's because of an accident, not because of a sickness.

Now let's **seal off the Critical Illness deductible, the vulnerable spot** on the bottom left of the triangle.

The other 13% - 14% of the time, if you or a family member ends up in the hospital, it's going to be because of a critical illness (cancer, heart attack, stroke, kidney failure, etc.).

The Critical Illness part of your plan will pay you a lump sum amount to cover your deductible and your out-of-pocket expenses. Any amount over your deductible ($5K up to $245K) can go toward your daily living expenses while you are recovering from your critical illness.

Now you can understand the reasoning behind the **Triangle Effect Strategy**. What **you have accomplished by using this simple, yet powerful strategy is to minimize your financial exposure in 98% to 99% of medical events either you or your family may experience.**

HOWEVER, you have one final question you may want to ask. What about the 1% to 2% that appears to fall between the cracks in this strategy? That is a great question that should be addressed!

Please keep in mind there is no one policy in today's market that will pay 100% of all medical events at all times. If there were, everyone would run to it and that company would close its doors because it would run out of money at lightning speed!

What are these typical, normal medical events that fall through the cracks? And, by falling through the cracks, I mean, the medical bill is not paid at 100%?

For a child or adult, it could be an appendectomy or tonsillectomy. The reason is an appendectomy and tonsillectomy are not the result of an accident and are not considered a critical illness. For an adult, it's gall bladder surgery or a hernia repair.

In these medical scenarios, as long as you are in-network, your provider's service bill would be sent to the insurance company. Your insurance company "re-prices" the bill to give you the lower contracted rate. In many cases the re-pricing may be anywhere from 50%, sometimes as high as 80%. In those cases, the re-priced amount is the only responsibility you have at that point in time if you have not met your deductible or your maximum out-of-pocket expenses.

Important: If you should need help in paying the 1% to 2% of potential medical events that may fall through the cracks, there are **Medical Billing Advocacy services** available for you throughout the country. These advocacy services will review all your medical bills for errors, overcharging, double billing, incorrect codes, and negotiate on your behalf.

Two (2) recent "real life" examples of success using the above Triangle Effect Strategy:

1. One of my clients, (we'll call him "Dave"), signed up with the above strategy I recommended to him. At the time Dave was approved with his health insurance, he was 52 years old, a non-smoker, was height/weight proportionate, but had been taking cholesterol medication for 2+ years.

   About 8 months into his health coverage with us, Dave suffered a heart attack. His health plan had $10,000 in critical illness coverage, was on an 80/20 major medical plan, had $10,000 in accident supplemental coverage, AND had a $10,000 deductible.

   Dave was upset and stressed since he was in the hospital and racking up a **sizable medical bill totaling $88,400** between his hospitalization, ambulance, surgery, medications, all diagnostic testing, cardiac specialists' consultations, and follow-up visits.

   Dave was out of work recuperating from his surgery and heart attack. Additionally, his wife was working making ends meet for their daily living expenses. But, Dave was very worried over the $10K deductible and his responsibility of another $3K in out-of-pocket expenses.

   Fortunately, the insurance company that issued his **Critical Illness Plan** sent him a check for $10K upon the diagnosis of his heart attack. We were also able to show the hospital that since Dave was not working, he and his wife were barely scraping by paying their daily living expenses.

The hospital "forgave" the $8,400 balance that Dave owed them as that was his deductible balance because his insurance company already paid $80,000 in re-priced bills. So, Dave had the extra $10K to use for his other daily living expenses (utilities, car payments, groceries, real estate taxes, etc.) and he was able to pay for his maximum $3,000 out-of-pocket expenses.

2. Another client we will call Steven. Steven is now 27 years old, a husband with two children under 3 years old. When Steven approached me to design his family's health care plan he was 25 years old. We reviewed all his options together and he felt the Triangle Effect Strategy was his family's best option package.

Since Steven played quite a bit of sports and was planning a larger family, he felt the Accident Supplemental portion of his plan was a great concept. He decided on a 100% coinsurance plan with both the Accident and Critical Illness supplements built into his family plan and a $5,000 deductible. That was a smart decision on his part!

About 6 months ago Steven was playing a friendly game of baseball. He twisted his right knee when running and the pain never stopped.

Within one week, Steven had knee surgery to repair his injury, went through eight weeks of physical therapy, has had over five physician visits, and is currently wearing a temporary knee brace. His medical bills totaled about $16,000. Since he has the Accident supplement already built into his health plan for $5,000, his first $5,000 in bills was paid by the Accidental coverage. In effect, this satisfied his deductible.

Then the 100% coinsurance kicked in after the $5K deductible had been paid. So, his remaining balance of $11,000 has been paid in full by the insurance company. The money out of Steven's pocket was ZERO. Is he happy? A resounding YES!

To conclude, the **Triangle Effect Strategy** is a proven, powerful method to strategically structure and design your health care plan so **national medical statistics work in your favor**, not against you. It empowers you and your family to obtain the best comprehensive major medical coverage at the lowest possible price.

About Frank

Frank Saltzburg is a Regional Manager and Partner at Healthcare Solutions Team whose corporate offices are located in Lombard, IL. He currently resides in Boca Raton, Florida. He holds the designation of a Certified Healthcare Reform Specialist (CHRS) and is a graduate of Rutgers University.

With over 20 years financial services, health care plan design, health care reform expertise, and management experience, Frank helps his clients obtain the health care coverage that best solves their needs. His expertise includes custom-designing affordable health care plans for individuals, families, and small business owners (under 100 employees). He holds licenses in Arizona, Florida, Pennsylvania, Ohio, California, Georgia, Nevada, Oregon, Washington, Texas, Alabama, North Carolina, Utah, and Idaho.

Frank has access to both the Private and Public Insurance Exchanges. He will determine if you are able to qualify for a tax credit/subsidy and receive your approval within 30 minutes meeting the ACA (Affordable Care Act) guidelines during open enrollment period. Additionally, Frank works closely on the Private Exchanges all year long and is well-known for designing the most comprehensive health care coverage plans based upon your needs, your family's, or your business needs.

Frank is also a keynote speaker on the current Affordable Care Act (aka Obamacare) and its impact on America's families and small businesses. He is the "GO-TO" person to make sure you are aware of all your options and strategies under the Affordable Care Act.

Email: fsaltzburg@gmail.com
LinkedIn: http://www.linkedin.com/in/franksaltzburg/
Website: www.ushcre.com
Phone: 561-756-8030

CHAPTER 9

IS THERE ANYTHING GOING ON IN MAY?
— A SIMPLE QUESTION WITH A LIFE-CHANGING IMPACT

BY KIM LABRECHE

I have always been told that I ask a lot of questions. The most popular question you'll hear from any child, of course, is "why?" When children ask this question, we as adults are patient (most of the time!) but what would happen if we, as a world nation, did not ask questions? Where would we be now?

For those of you who believe in the law of synchronicity and the law of attraction, we know that if *we* ask questions then *we* can set the wheels in motion to get what we want and desire. When we focus on watching for its manifestation and see the result unfold as confirmation, it becomes as easy as "putting in your order." However, there is one important and requisite ingredient inherent in the above. Can you think of what that may be?

FAITH!

We could choose to believe that it is as simple as asking for what we want, letting the request go, and waiting for the result to appear!

MY QUESTION AND POWERFUL CONFIRMATION

First, you need to know that I am an accountant—not your typical "bean counter" as we are more commonly known. I am an entrepreneur by nature with a very strong humanitarian focus. For those of you that have relationships with accountants, you know that all accountants are extremely busy during the March and April "tax season" every year, resulting in downtime in May.

Secondly, I hold a deep conviction that we are a part of many "communities" throughout the duration of our life. I believe in giving back to these communities whenever and wherever I can.

This story begins at Semiahmoo Rotary in South Surrey, British Columbia one fine Thursday morning in March of 2007. One of our Rotary members is the Executive Director of the Canadian Wheelchair Foundation. The previous November she had taken a group with her to Rosarito, Mexico, where they held "wheelchair presentations." The presentations educated community members about wheelchairs and gave them the opportunity to receive a wheelchair if required. The trip had an immense impact on the communities and the surrounding areas. After hearing their stories, I knew that I wanted to have that same experience – to also make a difference in people's lives.

Uncertain of the outcome, I decided to put my question out there. I had to find out if there was any chance that I might be able to make a difference in a community abroad. **"Is there anything going on in May?"** The answer I received was better than I could have expected. The Executive Director said, "Yes! In fact, the contact in Panama is wonderful. Let me get in touch with him for you." My heart immediately stopped as I thought that my simple idea to embark on a Rotary mission in May could actually turn into a reality. I looked around and saw a fellow Rotarian and asked if she would like to go along with me. As it turned out, we discovered that we could tag along with members of the Ontario Rotary, who were responsible for sponsoring the container of wheelchairs. Before we knew it, there were six of us from BC heading on an unforgettable journey to Panama.

While in Panama, we had the opportunity to see firsthand what the gift of mobility can give to individuals and their families. I must say, we witnessed some harsh conditions while presenting to individuals in remote communities. But little did I know that my own personal mission was not yet over….

Once the formal portion of our trip was done, our wonderful host told us about some excursion options that we could enjoy before returning to Canada. One of the excursions was the Panama Embera Indian Village Chagres River tour. Tourists go down the Chagres River in a dugout canoe manned by young natives, head into the rainforest for a swim and then return to the village where a chief speaks to tourists about their tribe, village and life. We decided to take part in this excursion. Our host's parting words to us were: **"Don't forget to ask if anyone needs a wheelchair!"**

What happened next is an order filled……..

The Embera indigenous tribe was one of five along the Chagres River that were established years ago by the local Government. Tours allow tribe members to sell their wares to tourists, and in turn, enable the tribe to grow as a community. With encouragement from my son, I had brought along many of his small stuffed toys to share with the children in the tribe. As I was handing out the toys, our tour guide tapped me on the shoulder and pointed me in the direction of a native woman who was standing next to her. The native woman handed me a necklace and asked me to give it to my son. She said it was a token of her gratitude for my son's kindness in offering to give his toys to the children. In that instant, a connection was made between two women from two very distant parts of the world!

Before leaving, I remembered to ask: **"Does anyone need a wheelchair?"** The expression on the chief's face was one of disbelief. The chief brought us out to his "hut on stilts" to show us his thirteen-year-old son who was lying on a bed. He was motionless. The tour guide explained that they believed the boy had suffered from meningitis at the age of two and now had to be physically lifted by tribe members when he needed to be moved.

A week later, I received pictures of a red wheelchair in a dugout canoe on the river. I also had the pleasure of seeing pictures of the red wheelchair as it went up the stairs of the native chief's home to be received by his son. When I saw these pictures I was overcome with emotion and gratitude. I often wished that I could have been there to see this epic event taking place. I would have loved to see all of their faces and to this day, I still get teary-eyed when I tell this story. I recently spoke with the Executive Director of the Canadian Wheelchair Foundation and was told that the young man who received the red wheelchair has since received a replacement wheelchair, as he had outgrown the original one. I was very grateful that my *simple question* had resulted in such a life-changing experience for a young boy and his community in a remote part of the world. To all those who were involved, I thank you.

So…what is the difference between a business owner that is overwhelmed with the demands of their business and one that has the freedom to ask big questions and step out in faith?

I. BUILD YOUR D.R.E.A.M. TEAM TO SUPPORT YOUR BUSINESS VISION

The privilege of undertaking humanitarian excursions, such as the one I took to Panama, is a result of having built a D.R.E.A.M. team of employees that support my business vision. As an entrepreneur, ask yourself what type of people you need in your business in order to feel supported in your goals. Share your business vision with your team members. Once you find the right individuals, mold the team to be self-sufficient. I have no doubt that if you have <u>faith</u> and <u>ask</u> for the D.R.E.A.M. team, the D.R.E.A.M. team will present itself to you.

D – DELEGATE – You will not be able to do it all! More importantly, if chosen wisely, your team members will want you to delegate to help them grow as professionals.

R – REWARD – Take every opportunity possible to express your appreciation for a job well done. Conduct "acts of kindness" towards clients or other team members and be as generous as you can. After all, they are indeed, your "business family."

E – EMPOWER – Provide team members the opportunity to take on responsibility and make decisions within defined parameters. Allow them the freedom to learn through their own experiences.

A – ACKNOWLEDGE – Celebrate team member's educational pursuits and family lives by being flexible with work schedules and time off. Trust me, when the time is right <u>for them</u>, they will come back. One of our team members called to ask if she could return to the team after a three-year maternity leave. Many other past employees still attend annual Christmas parties and group events!

M – MONITOR – We are still running a business. It is important to set measurable goals for your business and provide feedback to your employees – to let them know how they are doing.

II. "GUIDING FORCE" BUSINESS PRINCIPLES TO LIVE BY

a.) IT'S ABOUT THE MISSION – NOT THE MONEY
As entrepreneurs, we have all experienced our "business lessons." When we make it all about the money, our intentions are not for the benefit of both parties and as such are not "in balance." When we make it about the mission and focus our intentions

on how best to serve the other party, we are in fact ensuring the success of both parties and, as such, are "in balance."

b.) ACCEPT CLIENTS THAT ARE IN ALIGNMENT WITH YOUR CORE VALUES

At my accounting practice, our core values are displayed on all of our respective desks and at the front counter. Our core values are as follows:

- **Authentic relationships** – We want both parties to be comfortable being themselves.

- **Integrity and Respect** – Neither side should feel like they are compromising their ethics and are committed to quality work.

- **Team Focused Result** – The clients are getting a team of professionals and we all work together toward the common goal.

- **Friendly Environment** – We want clients to feel welcome when they visit us.

- **Learning Attitude** – We, and our clients, are committed to continuous learning.

c.) BE THE EXPERT TEAM – DO WHAT YOU LOVE AND LOVE WHAT YOU DO!

Clients value quality work and conducting business with excellence means you can sleep better at night. My team knows that I'm not satisfied until we've asked all the questions and we are certain that we completely understand an issue we are advising a client about. I have encouraged staff to specialize in areas they enjoy. We love the complexity of the world of accounting and tax, and as a result, partner with business owners to allow them the freedom to do what they love. Our passion for excellence helps us to build trust with our clients.

Our firm works with corporations, individuals, estates and trusts and non-residents of Canada. Our areas of accounting and tax expertise include:

- **Start-up businesses** – Should you incorporate? How will you keep records, pay yourself and generally monitor how your life changes from being an employee?

- **Growth companies** – How will you grow? What do you need to monitor? Will you have the need for new shareholders? Is it time to reorganize the corporate structure for more tax efficiency and better accumulation of wealth?

- **Succession planning** – What are your long-term goals? Is the corporate structure optimized for efficient tax minimization? Is the company ready for sale or is there more profit improvement needed? How valuable is your company and who should buy it? Are you transitioning the company to your family members?

- **Non-resident and cross-border issues** – Are you leaving or entering Canada, earning Canadian income as a non-resident with related withholding taxes, selling Canadian property as a non-resident or investing in US real estate through the use of US corporations?

- **Estates and trusts** – Is there an opportunity to minimize taxes and probate fees with the creation of trusts?

- **Personal tax** – Have you minimized tax with maximum use of tax credits and deductions? Have you considered dividends vs. salary as remuneration?

III. MY SUPPORTIVE LIFE PARTNER

Finally, if it were not for my loving husband who supports me in my entrepreneurial pursuits and my desire to be part of many "matters of the heart and soul" activities, I would not have been able to achieve such a successful accounting and humanitarian career. He brings a strong sense of humor and strength to our family, and plays a key leadership role at the accounting practice. He is a successful accountant with years of experience in industry and public accounting. I am truly grateful and blessed to have his love and support in both my personal and business life.

It is truly my vision to provide a caring environment for my team members and a positive experience for my clients!

SOME FINAL THOUGHTS.....

"What do you want to be when you grow up?" is another powerful question. Many of us have chosen to follow the same career paths as our parents. Yet, our world is full of ordinary people who dared to dream big. How do you think current world leaders such as Mark Victor Hansen, Jack Canfield, Peter Diamandis, Dr. Nido Qubein and Richard Branson (to name a few) answered this question? We know that these men are visionaries in their respective fields so their answers to this question would most certainly have included plans on a grand scale. They did not play small and had one thing in common - FAITH! They believed in themselves and had the confidence to realize what they set out to accomplish. Their successes now allow them the freedom to change the world and they are doing just that!

Wherever we find ourselves in life, we are offered opportunities to challenge the status quo and step out in faith. I am grateful that by asking a simple question at a Rotary meeting in British Columbia, Canada, I was able to make a difference on a grand scale in a Panama community. That being said, entrepreneurs can make a difference around the world everyday by sharing their big ideas and expertise. I recently had the privilege of going to Hollywood to receive my first Quilly award for my chapter: "Your Entrepreneurial Flight – Make it Happen" in the co-authored book, *Stand Apart* with Dan Kennedy. The royalties from *Stand Apart* are supporting causes around the world including Peter Diamandis' XProject for Global Literature. By sharing my entrepreneurial knowledge with others, I have been able to contribute to a global cause that speaks directly to who and what I am.

I know that my success was not a by-product of pure luck. I have intentionally surrounded myself with people who support me and share my pursuit of excellence in my business and personal life. I have given them opportunities to grow and together we have tackled the big questions. In doing so, we have been able to make an impact in the communities in which we are a part of.

So now, are there any questions that YOU have been waiting to ask?

About Kim

Kim LaBreche, CPA, CA and best-selling author, has worked with thousands of individuals, entrepreneurs and executors throughout her career in accounting and finance. Kim is the owner and managing partner of Saklas & Co. Chartered Accountants, a public accounting firm located in South Surrey, British Columbia, Canada.

Kim is passionate about making a difference in the lives of her clients and conducts "business with heart and soul." Her "Make It Happen" approach ensures that things get done efficiently, and her attention to detail in the delivery of her services is appreciated by those who work with her.

Kim has assembled her "D.R.E.A.M." team of professionals and supports her clients in areas of personal tax, corporate accounting, business succession, and complex tax optimization strategies utilizing trusts. Kim and her team work hard to assist business owners in maximizing their profits and minimizing their taxes. Her firm partners with entrepreneurs to help them navigate the complex world of accounting and tax, so they are free to focus their energy on what matters most to them. The firm's success is directly attributed to a commitment of providing quality service in a timely fashion.

If you are interested in working in partnership with a team of professionals who sincerely care about you and your accounting and tax needs, Saklas & Co. Chartered Accountants would love to hear from you!

Please visit our website at: www.saklasaccounting.com or reach us by phone at: 604-531-2292. Kim LaBreche and Saklas & Co. Chartered Accountants can also be found on Facebook, Twitter and LinkedIn. Start following them today!

CHAPTER 10

YOUR OWN FASHION BRAND IN 90 DAYS: WALKTHROUGH FOR HARDCORE GAMERS

BY JULIA ANTUFJEW

I am a passionate gamer. I love computer adventures the same way I love manufacturing fashion. A lifetime of gaming and manufacturing taught me: use a walkthrough when you are stuck. Game spoiler? I enjoy my games knowing what is coming next. I call it DEFINITE VISION. And yes, I still feel afraid and excited. But mainly I feel free of uncertainty, I feel as if I have already arrived.

Today I will walk you through a tough game play: launching your own fashion brand. Note: the game play varies from person to person. A few things are already decided upon once a new game starts, such as your COMMITMENT and SKILLS SET. You must save often in order to be able to reload.

[ENTER WALKTHROUGH ZONE NOW]

DAY 1: GAME CHARACTER
There are two choices really: you are either a warrior or a magician, either an entrepreneur or an artist. An entrepreneur finds a need and designs a product around it. The ultimate need of an artist is self-expression.

111

An entrepreneur starts in EASY MODE. The single product focus gives ultimate leverage at start, so they only need as much time and budget to develop and market one product.

Being an artist is much more exciting. An artist starts in HARD MODE but the end bonus is beyond any imagination.

DAY 2: TAKE YOURSELF SERIOUSLY

When I started my first company, in all excitement I called a friend and told her – "I am a CEO now!" "No, you are not" – she laughed – "You don't even have any employees." Back then I spent nights brooding about it: - "Is she right?" Now I know: if you say you are a CEO – you are one, so be one. Once character is chosen – live it. Take yourself seriously.

The same counts for your environment, your team, your partners, your systems, and your customers. You deserve the best; nothing less. You deserve a great working environment; bright, hard-working, cheerful team members; professional, quality-driven partners; systems functioning as precisely as atomic clocks and enthusiastic, grateful customers.

DAY 3: WEAPONS [YOUR GREAT PRODUCT]

Entrepreneur: Find a need – design a solution.

Artist: Define inspiration for your brand and your first collection. You need a sound story to inspire your fans and lead your manufacturer and creative team.

For any gamer counts: the story is far more important than product. You have 90 days to define and refine your unique story, the one making people live/love your brand.

DAY 4: PLAYGROUND [YOUR TARGET GROUP]

A target group is never "all women" and a market is never "the globe" to start with. Envision your customer. Is your product for men, women or children? What age? What are their reasons to purchase? What is the need your product addresses? Talk to your friends; gather as much feedback as possible. Refine your thoughts using Facebook Graph Search.

Do you have a groundbreaking new bra idea? Go to Facebook and find the fan page of an established bra brand similar to yours with a minimum of 500 followers. You will need to understand the general profile of your target group: age, gender and interests.

Age puzzle:
Type into search window: *women who like [BRANDNAME].* Once list is loaded, click on: *SEE MORE FILTERS* at the right side of your screen. Find *AGE RANGE*. Select the first age bracket: 18-22. Count, note. Follow the same procedure for all age brackets and for: *men who like [BRANDNAME]* key phrase. Once your numbers are done, check what age brackets account together for 50%-60% of the research population. For instance: women 18-29 years old account for 50% of: *women who like [BRANDNAME].* This is your initial target group in terms of age. In this exercise you work with a sub-group of FB users whose age is visible to the general public. We assume this sub-group is representative of the total population of *women vs. men who like [BRANDNAME]*.

Gender puzzle:
From the previous exercise, sum up all females and males who have stated their age and calculate gender %age from the group as a whole. From all people who are interested in a particular bra product, lets say 60% are female and 40% are male. Men 30-39 years old show the greatest interest in bra subject. Interesting finding, however it is not clear how to interpret male bra involvement as for now. I am sure the future bears a great epiphany. It is an adventure, remember? So for now, your best guess is that women accounting for 60% of the research population are your initial stakeholders. This is a fun game. A brain twister it is!

Interests puzzle:
Type into search window: *Favorite interests of women who like [BRANDNAME].* Note as many interests as you think make sense. This list may give you the first rough idea about your customers' social profile.

Geographical location:
At the beginning of your path, your own country is your strength. Next to in-depth understanding of own culture and language, you have a major logistics advantage of being able to fulfill orders directly from your home.

DAY 5: THE TAO OF TIMING
Stores will buy from you either in February – March or August - September. Any other time – budget spent, queue up.

Live by international fashion calendar.

Fabrics selection	Twice a year: February & September.
Product development	Twice a year. February – June. September – December.
Shooting/Catalogue	Twice a year. January & July
Product presentation	Twice a year to wholesale: February - March, August - September.
Order placement:	April & October for wholesale/Flexible schedule replenishment orders.
Bulk manufacturing	April – July and October – January for wholesale/Flexible replenishment.

A sound plan is THE KEY to your success. PLAN!

DAY 6: BUDGET
An artist and entrepreneur would need approximately and respectively $15,000 and $5,000 to launch their brand including product and packaging development, shipment, logotype, annual domain hosting, annual website fee, product shooting and catalogue, and initial stock of respectively 72 units (24 styles, 3 pieces per style, 3 sizes) and 60 units per product. This calculation does not include trademark registration, company

establishment, advertising, trade show and fashion weeks participation.

DAY 7: REST

DAY 8: PRICE RESEARCH
Go to local boutiques and on-line stores carrying product similar to yours, note prices. Draft your target retail prices for various product categories based on those findings.

DAY 9: TEXTILES
Textiles inspire!

Entrepreneur: submit your idea to manufacturer for implementation advice including your target retail price. Entrepreneur products are often technical and require specific textiles to perform. Receive advice and swatch cards.

Artist: Visit local or international textile fairs for inspiration. Gather as many swatches as you can. For efficiency-oriented designers – order from an on-line textile library. A great textile library is carried by: www.quantumfactory.net. You will need about 60 swatch cards to make your wildest dreams come true.

DAY 10: MANUFACTURER
You may need more than one day to find a manufacturer, so start early. You need a reliable manufacturer with no minimum order quantities, who in the best case can source your fabrics and trims.

DAY 11-16: CREATION
Make a blueprint of your great product or fashion sketches for your collection. Write down detailed description of your garment. How many styles? An average boutique would need about 12 styles of one brand to fill the rack. Given a 50% chance that a particular buyer likes a particular style, you would need minimum of 24 garments. Your styles have to form fantastic looks. The more looks you can create with 24 styles, the better. Draw 50 styles, select 24 best. A little cheat for artists – make

lots of dresses. A dress is a look by itself. Entrepreneurs need one great product.

DAY 17: SIZING
Go online and search for sizing tables of established brands serving similar target group as yours, download, discuss with your manufacturer.

DAY 18: CRAFT QUOTE
Inquire for bulk FOB pricing for various order quantities. Add to your pricing template.

DAYS 19-20: SWATCH CARDS ARRIVE
Sit down with your entire card collection and drawings, look at them, feel them, and allocate textiles to garments. Pay attention to textile prices. 5% of your garments may be very special and expensive, 20% - special and medium-priced and the remaining 75% super wearable and affordable. Give SKU numbers to all creations; compile tech packs on garment level including drawing, garment description, textile numbers and size requirements. Use the same fabrics for as many garments as possible without compromising design.

DAY 21: FABRICS CONSUMPTION
Calculate fabrics consumption as raw garment length plus sleeve length. Add fabrics consumption and costs into pricing template on SKU level.

DAY 22: BULK ORDER FREQUENCY
Bulk order frequency may vary from 2 consolidated annual orders up to 52 orders placed every Monday.

Less annual orders decrease your project management and manufacturing costs, while increasing the total inventory investment and inventory-associated risks.

I recommend an initial stock level of 3 pieces per style (all three in different sizes), weekly replenishment frequency for artists and 60 units initial inventory, monthly replenishment frequency for entrepreneurs as a lean entry model. Initial stock is important to facilitate direct sales to friends and fans, send garments to fashion magazines for shootings and distribute salesmen samples. Do not underestimate your friends and fans. For the first two seasons, they will be your most stable cash flow source. Artist: once a piece is sold – you place replenishment order to arrive 14 days later. Entrepreneur: Place a replenishment order every month. Order volumes depend on your monthly sales volumes.

DAY 23: PRICE LIST

Your ultimate goal is to turn your manufacturing price 2.5 times on average for wholesale plus 3 times in retail. 150 pieces per style per color are required to get there. Until then:

Pieces per style/color	Mark up wholesale	Mark up retail
3	1.5	2.5
20	2	2.5
60	2.5	2.5
150	2.5	3

Finalize your pricing template and compile a price list for buyers.

DAY 24: SAMPLE METERS AND PROTOTYPING

Order textiles to be shipped directly to your manufacturer. Place product development and initial inventory order.

DAYS 25-26: CHARACTER NAME

Your brand name may evolve. Often the first two names of your choice are already taken. Look up your name in the trademark register of your country. Check whether domain is still available. Both .com and .net score best with global search engines.

DAYS 27-30: WEBSITE

Consider all-in-one e-commerce solution by one of major platforms. You can operate under a sub-domain, until your own domain is secured, writing your content and determining your online strategy.

DAYS 31-37: MODELS AND PHOTOGRAPHER

Imagery is of key importance. It has to look fabulous. Find a photographer with a great fashion portfolio. Ask your photographer to refer you to a great modeling agency and catalogue editor.

DAYS 38-40: TRADE AND FASHION SHOWS PLANNING

Participation in at least 2 trade shows and fashion weeks a year is necessary to put your brand on the fashion map. Find suppliers who organize trade show and fashion week participation for a group of designers, where the costs are shared by all participants.

DAYS 41-43: GRAND OPENING PLANNING

The Grand Opening is the day when you launch your brand. Secure as much friends' help as possible. You will need a venue and a crowd to attend: friends, friends of friends, bloggers, media and storeowners. Research venues suitable for a runway. Research fashion bloggers, media and storeowners in your area. Make an invitee list and brand presentation scenario. You need: slide show projector to project your pictures, 2 models to present your garments, well-lighted runway area, display area for your garments, fitting space, drinks and music. Advertise in local media. If well-organized, retail sales during Grand Opening will cover the organizational expenses.

DAYS 44-45: SALES STRATEGY

Sell both retail and wholesale, to establish respectively short-term cash flow and long-term credibility. Make a list of all people from your networks who may be interested in your product. Make the list of all stores in your area where you want your product to be sold.

DAYS 46-52: LOGO

Write a sound briefing and outsource your logo development at: www.fiverr.com.

DAYS 53-54: TRADE MARK AND DOMAIN

Register.

DAYS 55-56: SOCIAL MEDIA
Set up Facebook, Pinterest, Twitter and Instagram accounts.

DAYS 57-67: REMAINING 10,000 THINGS

DAY 68: PROTOTYPES ARRIVE
You have been talking to your manufacturer daily for past six weeks. You have seen pictures of your garments and have given adjustments feedback. Finally the carton boxes arrive. Take a deep breath and open the box. Fit all styles on your fitting model who may as well be yourself or your friend. Make pictures and improvements notes. If necessary, revise your look combinations for fashion shooting.

DAYS 69-70: CASTING
You will need a model. Shooting using friends may seem like a great idea, but it is not. People need great inspiration. What they do not need is a reflection of what they already are.

DAY 71: SHOOTING
Shoot at least 8 fashion pictures for your lookbook and three pictures per look for line sheet: front, side and back.

DAYS 72-75: LOOKBOOK AND LINE SHEET
Combine lookbook and line sheet into one catalogue. Add SKU number, garment name and available color combinations under each picture. Catalogue and price list are main vehicles of product communication to your buyers.

DAYS 76-77: INVITATIONS FOR GRAND OPENING
Send out invitations. Ask for RSVP. Send out a reminder 7 days before the event.

Day 78: WEBSITE UP-LOAD
Up-load your pictures to your website and social media.

DAYS 79-89: CATALOGUE TO BUYERS
Send out catalogue and price list to local buyers, call to confirm receipt. Make sure they attend your grand opening.

DAY 90: GRAND OPENING

Write to me about this day. If you have done everything with passion – you will be placing your replenishment order on DAY 92.

(Why not DAY 91? Because even the greatest fashion designer deserves a day of rest!)

ANY DAY: GAME OVER? RESTART!

I am sure you have heard this song before:

- Impossible! Impossible! It is far more than that!
- You have to work for at least a full 11 years to launch a fashion brand!
- It's only for creative minds that learned design in school!
- Impossible! Impossible! Comply! Obey the rule!

Don't comply. Start to succeed. Failure as opposed to death is merely an option. Save frequently to be able to reload. Save 10% of everything you earn. There will be enough people drafting sophisticated charts on cafeteria napkins demonstrating all various reasons for your future failure. General game rule: pretend to listen while running away! Unless … the person you are talking to is a greatly successful gamer playing same character as you do. Then – listen, learn, and adjust.

It takes more than 90 days to become a fashion star. This path is for the warriors and magicians among us, fully committed, for those who just don't give up. No matter how long it takes – if fashion design is THE WAY OF YOUR HEART – you will walk it full of joy, happiness and satisfaction.

Every time you think GAME OVER – I say RESTART! I say START!

About Julia

Julia Antufjew is one the key characters in the rapidly-growing Fashion Incubator also known as: QUANTUMFACTORY.NET. Julia's mission is to empower 10,000 emerging fashion designers launching their brands. Magic powers: Action, Great Team and Clear Vision. Julia and her team facilitate emerging fashion designers to start their brands from zero and to succeed in their venture. Julia teaches designers the main principles or the game play, runs in-house product development and manufacturing of designer's portfolio, and manages several distribution channels.

German, born in Russia, Julia travelled the world to make a stop in Shanghai/China and to found QUANTUMFACTORY.NET: a garment factory specializing in high quality designer wear.

Fascinated by creation, Julia developed a hands-on lean market entrance program for emerging designers minimizing initial investment – while securing revenues from the very moment of the brand launch. Graduate of Rijks University of Groningen, Fashion and Business Professional, Member of America's PremierExperts™, CEO of the most promising fashion venture and recently an author.

You can connect with Julia at:
julia.antufjew@quantumfactory.net
WeChat: Julia Antufjew
LinkedIn: https://cn.linkedin.com/in/juliaantufjew
Skype: tufatufa

CHAPTER 11

SALES EXCELLENCE – SEVEN STEPS TO ACHIEVING EXTRAORDINARY SUCCESS IN SALES

BY RICHARD TYLER

I have discovered over the years that the people who are the world-class sales professionals have one key characteristic in common, *commitment.* Achieving success in life always requires an extraordinary level of effort. This chapter is based on the premise of excellence, and excellence cannot be achieved and maintained without focused *commitment* combined with deliberate and continuous action to make it a reality.

In this chapter, you will discover an abbreviated version of my Tyler 7™ Steps to Sales Success. In my book *Sales Excellence – Seven Steps to Achieving Extraordinary Success in Sales* as well as our world-renowned Sales Immersion™ sales training course, we go into greater depth to teach these proven success principles. These steps are the critical elements that must be mastered by any Sales Professional that desires excellence. You will find there is nothing magical about these steps. However, what will seem magical are the incredible results you will achieve when you have mastered them.

THE TYLER 7™ STEPS TO SALES SUCCESS

Step 1 – Prospecting: Searching for new ways or opportunities to do business.

Consistent prospecting is the oxygen of the sales process because it is so often what breathes new life into a tough month, quarter or even year. Yet, prospecting is one area that many salespeople dislike. The "average" salesperson spends less than 10% of the day prospecting because they equate prospecting with cold calling, and they equate cold calling with rejection.

If you want to be better than average you have to get beyond call reluctance. You can do this, first, by saying to yourself, "MAKE THE CALL!" every time you think of a reason not to make the call. Then, immediately force yourself to make the call. In short order, your call reluctance will diminish and your success will rise.

Once you have identified your prospects, create a strategy for contacting them. For example, you can set aside one hour every day to make prospecting calls. Schedule who you will call during that time and schedule more than you can get to so you always have enough to fill your call time. Record the result of each call. By consistently tracking your prospecting you will quickly learn what you need to know to become significantly more effective. Those who successfully use a prospecting system have long forgotten the term "cold calling." Instead, they see themselves as discovering new customers. Accept that you will not always reach people or get a "yes" every time. This is part of the process. If you keep applying and improving the process, the Law of Averages will work for you.

Remember, you are looking for the "YES" among "NOs". When prospecting, I like to keep in mind something the great Andrew Carnegie, America's first great industrialist, said nearly 100 years ago when asked by a reporter how he managed to have 43 millionaires working for him. Carnegie informed the reporter that none of them were millionaires when he hired them. He stated that, "You develop millionaires the way you mine gold. You expect to move tons of dirt to find an ounce of gold, but you don't go into the mine looking for the dirt—you go in looking for the gold." That sage advice holds true for Prospecting.

Step 2 – Contact: The proper way to engage your customers.

When you meet your prospective customer, smile confidently, look them in the eye, greet them enthusiastically and shake their hand firmly. When you view every interaction as an opportunity to build a positive relationship, then you will become a more effective Sales Professional.

When you are getting to know your prospect, keep in mind that everyone requires a different amount of evidence before they believe something to be true. They will also have varying levels of trust with you. I call this the Evidence Factor™ and the Trust Factor™. The excellent Sales Professional will assess each and respond accordingly.

The illustration shows that a person's Trust Factor™ and Evidence Factor™ are inversely proportional. When there is greater trust, there will be a lower need for evidence. Conversely, when there is a lower level of trust, there will be a greater need for evidence.

You can begin to build trust and lower the amount of evidence by building rapport. Start by having a few questions ready to ask before you arrive at your appointment. For example, if you know he has just returned from vacation, ask how it went. If you know your prospect has recently received a promotion, ask what he/she did to achieve that goal. You get the idea. When prospects share information, it automatically begins lowering their defenses and creates a stronger base for developing a long-term relationship.

Step 3 – Wants and Needs Analysis™: Asking the appropriate information-gathering questions.

A proper Wants and Needs Analysis™ is the most critical component of the entire selling process. If you really understand your customers' wants and needs and you can help them, then you are no longer *selling* – you are *solving*. People don't like to be "sold," but they do like having their "problems solved." Helping them see how your product or service can meet their needs, satisfy their wants and solve their problems is your most important job.

Conducting a proper Wants and Needs Analysis™ does not have to be complicated, however it does take preparation. Your questions should help your customer to understand that you are interested in them, their business and solving their problems.

As a general rule, after you have successfully completed your initial greeting and rapport building, Tyler's First Six™ are among the first questions you should ask. Fully explore these questions with your customer. The answers will guide you to if, when and how you will be able to assist them.

Tyler's First Six™

1. How much time do you have available for our discussion today?
2. What do you know about (our company name)'s current capabilities?

3. What is the biggest problem facing your company (you) today?

4. How does that problem affect you and your responsibilities?

5. What are the most important objectives and goals for you in the next few years?

6. How soon will you need a solution to start working for you?

After you have successfully gained in-depth answers for Tyler's First Six™ from normal conversation, you should then continue the discovery process with Tyler's Following Five™.

Tyler's Following Five™

1. What type of budget considerations do we have?

2. What type of budgetary process will be used?

3. If we were fortunate enough to find something that fits both your solution and budget considerations, would you be in a position to proceed right now?

4. Beside yourself, who else will be involved in making this decision?

5. How do you normally handle the financial arrangements on product/service investments? (i.e., purchase orders, invoicing, terms, etc.)

These questions are designed to get at the heart of your customer's need and how decisions are made so you can develop a game plan for the rest of sales process. The answers to Tyler's First Six™ and Tyler's Following Five™ are not the only questions you will need answers to. They are just the beginning. You will need to determine what additional questions will be necessary. Remember, the answers will help you craft a solution.

Step 4 – Presentation/Demonstration™: The explanation of and customer involvement with the Features, Advantages and Benefits of your products and services.

Your goal is to help solve problems and satisfy wants and needs for your customer. To do this, you require in-depth knowledge of your products and/or services and their capabilities. In your preparation process, think through all the customer's potential objections or concerns. If you are prepared, you will be able to creatively assist your customer.

The explanation of, and customer involvement with, the Features and Advantages of your products/services in terms of Benefits to your customer is the core of any excellent Presentation/ Demonstration™. Most salespeople are good at Features and Advantages, but fall short on explaining Benefits. They assume the customer will draw the connection to the Benefit(s). However, that is not normally the case. If you can effectively show your customer how your product or service will provide a solution to their problem, you will be well on your way to a sale.

Step 5 – Resolution: Effective use of your knowledge to answer questions and resolve concerns.

If you properly anticipate concerns you will be adequately prepared to resolve them when they arise. Concerns are opportunities to further underscore the strengths of your solution. If you know what concerns to expect and how to handle them, you will find yourself reaching agreement much more often than you thought possible.

Below are **The Tyler 6™ - Power Resolution Steps**™ to help you uncover and resolve concerns:

1. **Listen to the concern** – Don't begin responding to the concern before the customer has the opportunity to express it fully.

2. **Give the concern back** – By repeating back the concern you will be able to verify that you have heard and understood the concern. It will allow the customer the opportunity to clarify and further explain if necessary.

3. **Investigate the concern** – Sincerely ask the customer to explain the concern in as much detail as possible. Gather

specific information as to what does not meet their wants and needs.

4. **Resolve the concern** – Use your skills, product knowledge and understanding of your customer's wants and needs to gain agreement on your solution.

5. **Verify the answer** – Once you have fully responded to the customer's concern, verify that your customer heard, understood and agrees with you. This can be accomplished by asking some simple questions like: "That clears up any concern you had, doesn't it?"; "This answer will solve the concern, won't it?"

6. **Disengage** – Signal your customer that you are moving ahead by speaking and using body language. Move your body, change your position and use statements like, "Let's turn our attention to…" or "I want to make sure I'm cognizant of your time so I'd like to move to…."

By implementing these key steps you will identify the concern and respond appropriately without detracting from your presentation.

Step 6 – Agreement: The determination to invest in your products and/or services.

Reaching agreement is what every sales person wants to achieve – however many struggle in this area.

The Tyler 5 – Agreement Line Up™ will guide you through this process.

1. Understand your customers' wants and needs

- Use probing questions constantly
- Probe their ability to pay
- If they reject something, investigate why
- Understand their motives
- Understand their values

- Be sincere

2. Recognize investment signs

Investment signs are not always a statement of commitment. They come in two other forms.

Verbal:

- They begin asking more questions
- They want more technical data
- They begin talking about how they would use the product/ service
- They start sounding more agreeable

Visual:

- Smiles
- Excitement
- Appearing to be more anxious
- Asking for another Presentation/Demonstration™

3. Make the decision for your customer

If you have done a proper Wants and Needs Analysis™, you should have enough information to give professional guidance to your customer on what to do.

- Lead your customer to the decision with questions
- Concentrate on the Features, Advantages and Benefits that are important to the customer, not to you!

4. Be assumptive, be casual

- Assume the customer is moving ahead with the Agreement
- Casually write the order
- Answer the concerns
- Resume the Agreement step

5. Remain natural

Many sales are lost because the salesperson has not practiced Agreement methods enough to feel or act confident and natural. Remember, in front of your customer is not the time to practice!

- Do not change your style
- Do not change your pace
- Remain relaxed
- Remain confident
- Remain alert

By understanding and practicing the **Tyler 5 – Agreement Line Up**™ you will find your Agreement ratio going up along with your revenue.

<u>Step 7</u> – Follow-through: An overlooked component to the sales process.

Reaching agreement doesn't mean the process is over. Focus on four components when following-through.

1. Provide additional customer service

Every time you provide additional customer service you open up more opportunities to learn about your customer's business. This knowledge will allow you discover more problems to help solve. In addition, you will develop a stronger relationship with your customer. The stronger the relationship, the less likely your competitors will draw them away.

2. Test for satisfaction

From time to time there will be customer satisfaction issues. Instead of running away, fix it. Studies have shown that 95% of dissatisfied customers would do business with a company again if their issues were solved quickly and satisfactorily. In fact, quickly and satisfactorily solving an issue increases customer loyalty.

3. Prospect for additional business

The most efficient way to develop new business is with old business. Once you understand your customer's business you have a great opportunity to propose new products and services. By using probing questions and leveraging your relationship you will often find needs you had not previously uncovered.

4. Prospect for referral business

A referral from a satisfied customer gives you immediate credibility and reduces the cost associated with prospecting. Here are a few tips to help you get the referral.

Be honest

Tell them you value their assistance and you know they could probably recommend two or three people who would benefit from your products and/or services. If the customer doesn't want to provide that information, tell them you respect their position and drop it.

Always Ask

Make it a point to always ask. Know what you're going to say and how you are going to say it. Remember, most people are quite comfortable providing referrals if satisfied.

Always follow-through

If you get a name, make the contact. It's not unusual for a salesperson to never contact the referral they were given. Respect the information you have been given and make the contact.

Always thank the customer for the referral

Regardless of whether the referral turns into business, make sure you thank the customer with a note or a phone call. Many times I have received additional prospects from my customer while I was thanking them for the previous prospects.

Always share the success

If one of the referrals you receive generates business for you, do something for your referring customer. It can be as simple as a gift card to a favorite coffee shop or even a book. These small gestures of appreciation let your customer know you sincerely appreciate their efforts.

Excellence in sales or any other aspect of life is within your grasp, but it takes hard work to achieve it. You have the ability. I encourage you to take the principles I have shared with you and make a difference in your life and in the lives of others.

Remember, your success tomorrow is in direct proportion to your 'Commitment to Excellence®' today™. ~ Richard Tyler

About Richard

Richard Tyler is the CEO of Richard Tyler International, Inc.® as well as a diversified family of successful companies and services.

Richard is a highly acclaimed speaker, trainer, consultant and author. He has earned a worldwide reputation for his powerful educational methods, motivational techniques and success training. His background in sales, leadership, management, customer service and quality improvement has allowed him to become one of the world's most sought-after consultants, lecturers and teachers. Richard shares his success and *Excellence* philosophies with millions of individuals each year through keynote presentations, writing, radio, television, seminars, books, CDs and web-based programs.

Richard has authored or co-authored over a dozen books with top experts such as: Mark Victor Hansen, Stephen Covey, Brian Tracy, Ken Blanchard, Denis Waitley, Dr. Warren Bennis, General Alexander Haig, Alan Keyes, Dr. John Gray, Ty Boyd, Dr. Robert Schuller and many others. Richard was selected as one of *America's PremierExperts™* and his philosophies have been featured in *Forbes* magazine, *Entrepreneur* magazine, *The Business Journals, Sales and Marketing Management* magazine, *Wealth & Finance International* magazine, *Acquisition International* magazine, the *Houston Chronicle* as well as in hundreds of articles and interviews. Richard has been seen on FOX, CBS, NBC and ABC television affiliates, CNBC.com, Morningstar.com, BostonGlobe.com, Moneywatch.com, MiamiHerald.com, Wall Street Journal's MarketWatch.com, YahooFinance.com and many others.

Richard's recognition and awards include: the *"Distinguished Speaker Award"* from the School of Business Administration at the University of Houston, *Who's Who Worldwide of Global Business Leaders,* the American Biographical Institute *"Man Of The Year Award"*, *Who's Who in American Education* and the *Outstanding Young Men of America Award* to name a few. "Keeping America Strong" a special 30-minute addition of "Heartbeat of America", a national television program hosted by William Shatner and Rear Admiral Kevin F. Delaney (ret.) featured Richard and Richard Tyler International, Inc®. Richard received the coveted *"Keeping America Strong"* Award for outstanding contributions to the strength and growth of American Business.

Richard's "Commitment to Excellence"® *Sales Immersion™, Leadership Mastery™,* and *Excellence in Quality and Service™* programs have been taught at the university level and Richard serves as a Master Trainer to students at The Center for Entrepreneurship at Houston Community College.

Richard is a contributing writer to LinkedIn's Pulse News and is a Mentor in the "LinkedIn For Good" Mentorship Program For Veteran Job Seekers. Richard servers on the Advisory Board and is past Chairman of Be an Angel Fund, a charity that helps children with multiple disabilities and profoundly deaf children to have a better life.

Richard Tyler International, Inc.® has been recognized as one of the top training and consulting firms in the world. Among it's numerous honors are *"Top Sales Training and Management Consulting Firm in the United States"*, the *"Best For Corporate Growth Strategy – USA"*, the *"Award for Excellence in Sales Training – USA"*, *Management Consultancy of the Year* and the *"Best of Business Award"* Management Consultancy.

As Richard says:
Remember, your success tomorrow is in direct proportion to your 'Commitment to Excellence®' today.™

You can connect with Richard at:
RichardTyler@RichardTyler.com
www.RichardTyler.com
www.SalesImmersion.com
www.linkedin.com/in/RichardTyler
www.facebook.com/RichardTylerInternational
www.twitter.com/RichardTylerInt
https://plus.google.com/+RichardTyler/posts
Tel: (+1) 713.974.7214

CHAPTER 12

FINANCIAL PILLARS TO BUILD WEALTH FOR THE FAMILY

BY BIBI BUNMI APAMPA

We all have dreams of being financially independent with a desire to build wealth for future generations. This does not have to remain a dream. This dream can be turned to reality.

There is a five-step process that we will need to follow for early realization of the dream of being financially independent with wealth that your family can continue to enjoy in the future.

1. Saving Money – Save and invest part of your earned income and turn it into capital.

2. Own a Business – Turn that capital to enterprise by starting a business to escape from a fixed pay scale.

3. Diversification – Turn the profit from the enterprise into financial freedom by investing in real estate.

4. Leverage – Grow financial base by building multiple streams of income generating assets.

5. Delay Gratification – Use only the income generated from your assets to buy your luxuries; do not use your capital.

We can build multiple passive income streams using the Four Pillars of Wealth. I call them pillars because they share some

137

of the same attributes of pillars we see in homes, municipal buildings, and ancient structures such as the Parthenon in Greece that still stand today.

FOUR PILLARS OF WEALTH

Invest in seven ventures, yes, in eight; you do not know what disaster may come upon the land. Ecclesiastes 11:2 NIV

The Four Pillars of Wealth are:

1. Real Estate
2. Portfolio Investments
3. Business Enterprise
4. Expert Domain

I. Pillar of Wealth - Real Estate

One undeniable habit of millionaires is that regardless of how they make their money, they always keep their wealth in real estate. Real estate is the preferred pillar that people use in the pursuit of building sustainable family wealth and passive income stream. Income from real estate is a sustainable wealth stream that can be handed down to future generations.

Financial Independence using real estate strategies is possible by being prudent in sourcing for properties in good locations and buying one investment/rental property every two to three years.

Here is a list of the real estate investments you can get involved in:

1. Your Home – Your home is one of the largest and most important investments you will make in your lifetime. This should serve as the starting point in creating Wealth for the family. A home that is eventually free of debt is one of the biggest assets you can leave your children. Try to pay off the mortgage early by making extra payments. You can use

the equity in your home to make down payments for other investment properties.

2. Buy to Let – These are homes you buy as investment property specifically for rental income. The key to success in this strategy is in the location of the property, which must be easily accessible by car and public transport, good security, and if possible, proximity to shops and good schools.

3. Housing for Multiple Occupancy – This is a house where you let out the rooms to different individuals instead of one tenant; you can buy a multi-unit building or convert a big house into rental units.

4. Commercial Property – These are properties used basically for commercial purposes like shops, offices, factories or warehousing. The advantage of investing in this kind of property is that long-term tenants (as with most businesses) don't like changing their address once they are well established at a location.

5. Land Speculation – Instead of buying landed property you can buy virgin land at a good location with the expectation that the value will rise over time, and you can sell it in the future at a profit.

6. Buy, Renovate, Sell – You buy a property that is either old, run down or needs repair, you renovate it to enhance its appeal, presentation and appearance. The property is then sold it for a healthy profit. This strategy would need an investor that either has a passion for interior decoration or property-renovation skills.

7. Lease Options – There are people that would love to buy a property or their own home, but cannot obtain a mortgage. In a lease option arrangement, the tenant puts down a down payment and a portion of the rent goes toward the purchase of the house. The house gets transferred to the tenant after the full payment for the house is made – as stated in the lease option agreement.

II. Pillar of Wealth - Portfolio Investments

The second pillar of wealth is built around a consistent savings culture combined with the miracle of compound interest - while investing excess funds in financial instruments - to build what is called portfolio income. Here is a short list of investments into which you can begin to invest your savings and watch it grow:

1. Savings accounts and fixed deposits – This is the starting point. Aim to save at least 10% of your income, which, if well invested overtime, can make you a millionaire. You can become a millionaire just by saving specific sums monthly detailed like the example below. You could build about $1,033,625 financial base in the following time frames:

   $100 per month – 3.30 per day @ 10% over 45 years

   $266 per month – 8.86 per day @ 10% over 30 years

   $759 per month – 25.30 per day @ 10% over 25 years

   $2422 per month – 83.30 per day @ 10% over 15 years

It's a good idea to start your savings plan today, as every day you delay is like burning up your financial future.

2. Investment in Shares and Stocks of companies – There are three basic ways to invest in the stock market. You will need to decide which one is in line with your wealth building goals.

   (i). Long Term Investment: Good strategy if using the stock market to save for future needs by buying shares in blue chip companies for dividend income and capital appreciation of the shares.

   (ii). Day Trading: This involves buying and selling stocks within a single day. It can be very profitable, but you can also lose money fast. It is advisable to go in for a course in day trading before starting the business.

   (iii). Penny Stocks: These are low cost shares of small public companies and are considered quite risky. However, the potential returns are quite high if you can choose stocks that have a strong return.

3. <u>Pensions</u> – this could be a self-invested pension scheme or by companies for their employees. It is a good idea to take advantage of this as most companies would contribute about the same amount that is deducted from your salary into the pension fund. The average return on investments on pensions is about 6%, but this is a solid investment with lower risk than other types of investments.

4. <u>Life Insurance</u> – The average return on this type of investment is about 2.25% annually. Again this is another low risk investment.

5. <u>Forex trading</u> – This involves trading in currencies of different countries against one another in an attempt to make a profit on the ever-fluctuating foreign exchange rate. In other words, you would use one currency to buy a value of the other currency, based on the current exchange rate of the two. If the currency you hold increases in value and you eventually exchange it back, you would make money. Of course, if the currency you hold decreases in value, you would lose money.

It is advisable to take up a course in Forex trading before starting on this strategy.

The key to success in building wealth using portfolio investments is a person's ability to convert earned income into passive and portfolio income as quickly as possible.

III. Pillar of Wealth - Experts Domain

The third pillar of wealth is to grow a financial empire by building a lucrative platform as an expert author, speaker, consultant, coach, or trainer. The process involves becoming an expert in a niche and developing resources and products for sale in that niche, thereby creating a business product funnel.

People need to:

- Hear you through your Audio programs, CDs, Podcasts, Audio training programs, webinars, etc.
- Read you through your book as a published author.
- See you through your videos, training DVDs, and video podcasts.
- Experience you at a live program through seminars and workshops.
- Be impacted by your expertise through your coaching programs.

Here are some tips on how to position yourself intelligently as an expert:

1. Know your topic – Know your topic inside and out. Develop the perfect elevator pitch and as you begin booking speaking engagements, develop a knockout keynote speech.

2. Discover audience needs and challenges – When writing a book, a training program, developing a workshop or keynote speech, you need to know what frustrations or struggles your target audience is facing and how to overcome them. Target your information around that.

3. Create your solution – Once you determine what their struggle is, develop a service or product that will provide a solution such as a book, DVD, seminar, program, or coaching sessions.

4. Develop a professional website – Your catchy professional website needs to have information and resources that relates to the niche in which you are an expert, with an eye towards Search Engine Optimization (SEO) so that potential clients can find you easily.

5. Campaign and promote yourself strategically and consistently. You can do this through public appearances, press releases, article writing, etc.

6. Partner with others to get your message out. Get involved in joint venture arrangements. People working together to capture an audience is more lucrative than trying it on your own. You can offer packages that add value to each other's offerings.

7. Post free content to generate traffic and use social media. You can create short eBooks and articles about particular issues that are of interest to your target audience.

IV. Pillar of Wealth – Business Enterprise

The fourth and final pillar in building wealth for the family is starting a small business enterprise.

One of the richest men in the world, J. Paul Getty once said, "You must be in business for yourself. You'll never get rich working for someone else." It is a good idea to start your own business enterprise which can be a physical business run from home or office location, or it can be a business on the Internet.

As you grow your business, your family can become part of that business or you can hand it down to your children when you retire. This creates income for you today, and wealth for your family in the future.

Here are eight easy steps to start your business:

1. Develop an outstanding business idea. This can take time and you may talk to others to determine whether your idea is lucrative and what you would need to get started such as additional training, licenses, patents, certifications, etc.

2. Research the business. Once you have developed your idea, begin researching your competition. What do they offer? How you can compete? What can you offer that is different? How can you add value?

3. Name your business. Don't rush this, as naming is the first step in branding. Make sure that you check to see if the

name is being used by someone else. Be sure to register your business name with the patent and copyright office.

4. Decide on legal structure. Will you be a sole proprietor or will you have partners? Will you form an LLC? There are different types of tax advantages and protections that certain types of legal structures offer.

5. Write your business plan. This includes your business operation, financing, marketing strategy, SWOT analysis and your vision statement.

6. Determine where you are going to do business. If you have a brick and mortar business you may need licenses, permits and other expenses to set up the business. If you are an Internet business then spend the time to create the right website for the business.

7. Put together your professional team. This includes lawyers, accountants, and other consultants. These are the people that you will rely on to keep your business running smooth and growing.

8. Source your finance. Determine whether you will have other investors or whether you will need to secure a small business loan.

CONCLUSION: WISDOM NUGGETS

A combination of these pillars is a sure way to pave the road to financial freedom, and sometimes we need a little help on the way. Check: www.GrowingFamilyWealth.com for more information on building wealth for the family.

Here are some final thoughts:

1. Be a lifetime learner - The more you learn the more you earn.

2. You must work to build passive income while you grow income-producing assets.

3. Build a real estate portfolio. Every 2-3 years buy at least one "excellent" piece of real estate.

4. Create, build and grow your Internet presence to become web-famous – especially if you are concentrating on building the wealth pillars of the Experts domain or business enterprise.

5. Learn and consult professionals on how to protect your financial fortress and legally minimize your tax obligations.

6. Maintain an attitude of gratitude while honoring others.

About Bibi

Bibi Bunmi Apampa is a Business Mentor and Wealth Coach specializing in teaching Financial Empowerment, Wealth Creation and Business Breakthrough Strategies through her website, Coaching/Mentoring Programs and Public Speaking Engagements.

Bibi is the Director of The Empowerment Centre Ltd. She is a Chartered Accountant, a Fellow of the Institute of Chartered Accountants and a Fellow of the Chartered Institute of Taxation.

Bibi is an internationally sought-after Author, Entrepreneur, Inspirational Speaker, Trainer, Life Coach, Wealth Strategist and Investor who has helped many people improve their lives financially, physically, personally, spiritually and professionally.

By listening to Bibi Bunmi Apampa: You get a Super Wealth Coach, a Business Mentor and a Marketing Queen all in one! A unique and highly powerful combination!

www.BibiApampa.org

CHAPTER 13

THE SECRET TO SUCCESS . . . ?

BY ROBERT GOLDSMITH

So, you want to be a success? Well, who doesn't? But how do you do it? First, the good news: You're in America, the land of opportunity! America, where success is possible for anyone who desires it, spawning the age-old adage, "If I can only make it to America, the streets are paved with gold."

In spite of the economic challenges, America is still the greatest country in the world and the reason why people continue squeezing through fences, traveling on small boats, and risking their lives just to be here. No other country offers as much freedom and opportunity to pursue one's dreams and live an extraordinary life as does America. For that reason, you have likely never heard the expression, "If I can only make it to Bulgaria, I'll be rich."

Now, the bad news: America is the land of opportunity, not the land of entitlement. Wouldn't it be nice if our elected officials actually remembered this? However, the misconception is that success will simply show up at your front door. It does not! Well, that would be with the exception of winning the Publishers Clearing House sweepstakes, but even then, you would still have to complete the entry forms. The fact is, to achieve success YOU must take the initiative; otherwise, it's a moot point.

Throughout the years, a virtual plethora of methods have been employed to achieve extraordinary success. From the proverbial "go to school, get a good job, work hard, and move up the corporate ladder" to the J. Paul Getty plan: "rise early, work late, and strike oil." If the likelihood of striking oil isn't in the cards for you, then you'll need to go with "Plan B."

Now, the best part about life in the 21st century is the Internet, the one place where you can find almost anything at the click of a mouse. Where to begin? Well, that's easy. Simply place the cursor in the browser, left click, and then type "Amazon.com." Your objective, find that one book, that one CD, that one magical formula, the "Secret to Success."

Excited you are, as you begin your quest, fingers itching, heart racing, knowing that when you click that mouse, the answer you seek will appear right in front of you, that elusive recipe for success! This is so simple, you think to yourself, Why didn't I think of this before?

CLICK! You hit the search button, and there it is . . . or not. OMG! Much to your dismay, instead of the magic formula, you find 41,864 books, tapes, and CD's on the "Secrets to Success." Can you say, "Holy dilemma, Batman! What now?" Which one should you choose? How long will it take to sift through 41,864 results? Where does one begin to separate "rhetoric" from "reality"? And frankly, if all those "secrets" really worked, why isn't everyone rich?

THE ONE THING

In the 1991 award-winning movie City Slickers, starring Billy Crystal and the legendary Jack Palance, there is a scene in which Curly (Jack Palance) and Mitch (Billy Crystal) are riding horses through the countryside when Curly tells Mitch that the secret to life is just "one thing." However, in the movie, that one thing is never revealed. So allow me.

Regardless of your chosen field of endeavor, the secret to success begins with one essential ingredient, that one critical component, that one prerequisite to achieving the results you seek. And now for the first time, I am about to reveal it to the world! Ready? Drum roll, please . . . the secret to success is . . . Sales! Yes, that's what I said. "S-A-L-E-S!"

Now, I know what you're probably thinking. "Hmmm . . . Sales? That's the secret to success? *Are you kidding me!*" But actually, no I'm not. Indeed, the lifeline of any business starts by making a sale. No matter what service you provide or what products you offer, you cannot generate any income until you get the job, consummate the deal, or persuade someone to buy something. That, my friend, is called sales.

Unbeknownst to most, sales is "the oldest profession in the world." Yes, yes it is! (I'll let you think about that one.) And, some of the most successful people in America are salespeople. Sales offers the average person the possibility to earn an extraordinary income without any special or unique skills or expensive formal education. Anyone who sincerely wants to, can excel in sales.

Now, before suggesting that you don't even like salespeople, or that you have never sold anything in your life, the fact is we are all salespeople. When someone says they have never sold anything, I respond by asking them if they have ever been on a job Interview or asked someone out on a date. If their answer is "yes," and it always is, I enlighten them with the fact that at that very moment, they were selling. Whenever you are attempting to persuade someone to make a decision about anything, in that instant, you are selling.

Whether you want to admit it or not, you and I, the kid down the street, the lady next door, your waitress, even your doctor, we all sell, everyone sells! And so, there you have it . . . THE SECRET TO SUCCESS . . . IT'S SALES!

SHHH . . . DON'T TELL ANYONE . . . IT'S A SECRET!

Actually, there are no secrets, no magical potions, no silver bullets, no secret sauce . . . although there are a few "Golden Nuggets." On the other hand, there are several strategic, tactical methods you'll need to employ, methods you must become proficient at – to sell successfully. Whether you're selling real estate, life insurance, nutritional or weight loss products, or even soap; most of the strategies for achieving success or avoiding failure (similar, yet different) can be applied towards your business. The results you attain will be based initially on the quality of the products you offer, as well as the proficiency of the strategies you employ. It is in the proper implementation of these strategies where most people tend to fall short. Therefore, If you're not earning what you desire, it's likely: *You're Earning What You Deserve . . . And That Sucks.* ~ Robert Goldsmith (Friesen Press 2014)

WHY ME?

For more than three decades I have been a salesman. Well, actually, a financial planner. And, while I don't personally consider my profession that of a "salesman," as far as the perception of the profession goes, most people do. And, regardless of what is factual, "Perception IS reality to the perceiver." As financial planners, in order to help people help themselves, not only must we be adept at financial concepts, tax strategies, and products, but we must also be capable of assuring clients that the strategies we implement and the products we use are in their best interests.

Even more challenging is that almost every well-designed financial plan starts with or requires the purchase of a quality life insurance product. Yes, I said, life insurance! Often perceived as a "necessary evil," something no one wants to buy and certainly never hopes to use. Life insurance, notoriously considered a commission-driven sale. And, if that isn't bad enough, to add fuel to the fire, life insurance isn't really life insurance at all. Actually, it's "death insurance."

In its infancy, life insurance was only intended to pay someone else when you died. And if you're dead, who cares, right? Well, thankfully, most people do! The good news is that today, life insurance isn't just death insurance anymore. It can actually be used to pay for your healthcare, generate profits, create cash flow, reduce taxes, and even to improve the performance of your other assets. And, you don't have to die!

However, because of those aforementioned original perceptions, every successful financial planner must also be skilled at the "art" of the sale. Now, in addition to having worked with my own clients for more than thirty years, I have also mentored, coached, and educated planners and advisors across the country. Not surprisingly, I have been exposed to just about every conceivable scenario, and by default, every sales objection ever created.

Needless to say, not only have I mastered nearly every financial strategy and concept to be successful as an advisor, but I certainly know what it takes to excel in sales. If I can sell "death" successfully for more than thirty years, you would almost certainly have to agree that I have the experience to sell almost anything. It is my intention to impart some of the wisdom and techniques I've employed over the years. So just for you, I have whipped up my own personal recipe I call the "Essential Ingredients" for peak performance. Allow me to count down my top twelve. . .

Goldsmith's Dozen Essential Ingredients For Success:

12. ***Don't be a Hypocrite***: If you can benefit from the product you offer, buy it. Perhaps you should even become your first client. However, if you don't believe in the product, don't buy it, but don't sell it either.

"Do as I do, not as I say."

11. ***Develop your Elevator Speech***: If the key to being successful is truly the axiom, "whoever sees the most, earns the most," then you'll need to know how to turn conversations into opportunities. This requires that you have at least one prepared "Elevator Speech" available for use at a moment's notice. A good elevator speech is made up of approximately ten words that will motivate a person to want to do business with you.

"He who has a thing to sell, and goes to whisper in a well, is not as apt to get the dollars, as he who climbs the tree and hollers."

10. ***Employ the power of 3 and your A-B-C's***: Three new contacts daily will provide a lifetime of business. By generating at least three new conversations each and every day, even on your days off (can you say; "Elevator Speech"), you should create nearly nine hundred conversations each year. Then, as you master the art of getting referrals you will always be in business.

*Always think the A-B-C's – "**A**lways **B**e **C**onversing."*

9. ***Never Sell — Solve***: Contrary to popular belief, most sales presentations should be focused on solving problems, not selling products. Those that suck at sales normally spend too much time trying to sell, rather than trying to solve. The fact is, we buy products for what they do, not what they are. For example, we buy a drill because we need a hole, we buy a car because it can take us where we need to go, and we buy soap to get clean.

And . . . we buy life insurance because of what it can do, not for what it is. For all intents and purposes, almost everything purchased is done so to solve a need or a want.

"To be great, a salesman has to be a problem solver."

8. *Ask Questions:* Another important ingredient is the ability to discover what motivates your prospects, what makes them buy? The only way to determine this is by asking questions, the right questions. If you do, the odds are your prospects will tell you all you need to know about why they need or want what you sell. Therefore, your objective is to have them do most of the talking, and eventually they will sell themselves.

> *"Unless the questions are asked, it is unlikely you will complete the sale."*

7. *The Advance Close*: Before you invest significant time with a prospect, it is imperative you establish early on if there will be any roadblocks that will keep you from doing business. Find out, by using the "Advance Close." What is the advance close? Answer: just one more question.

> *"If you agree, that implementing my strategy*
> *(or purchasing my product) will improve*
> *what you are currently doing, is there anything that*
> *would prevent us from doing business?"*

6. *Ask for the business:* While asking for the business may require you to face possible rejection, at some point you absolutely must ask a prospect to do business. The fact is, if you never ask, you always have the same answer, and that would be . . . "no!"

> *"You can't get what you don't ask for."*

5. *Follow up and follow through*: Every meeting you have and every presentation you do, will not result in the consummation of a sale, particularly after the first meeting. Typically, most sales are only completed after the 3rd, 4th or even 5th contact. It is imperative you follow up with each prospect to determine if the opportunity to do business exists. Most prospects will not comprehend everything you've shared with them on your first appointment. Therefore, it is important to remember . . .

"The fortune is in the follow through."

4. ***Never Stop learning***: The most important investment you can make is in YOU! Believing you know all you can know is dangerous, as others will pass you by. The fact is, life's education is never ending and the same is true in business. It is always prudent to continue to invest time and money in your education. In this case,

"A penny saved can be expensive."
~ Robert Goldsmith

3. ***Become a Great Story Teller:*** People love stories. The fact is, it's much easier for a person to relate to a story than it is to be "pitched" a product. Stories can offer up "heartfelt emotions," while a pitch can appear to be cold and insincere. Learn how to tell the stories of your satisfied clients relative to your prospect's circumstances. If you don't have one, borrow one from your upline, mentor, manager or associate until you have some of your own.

"Your Best Story begins when you start to tell them."
~ Robert Goldsmith

2. ***Find a Great Mentor***: Finding someone who "has been there and done that", is easy. Finding someone of that caliber, who is also willing to coach, train and mentor you . . . that, as they say, is "priceless."

Tiger Woods, arguably the greatest golfer to walk the planet, has a "swing coach." That's someone he pays big dollars to, just to watch him swing a golf club. He watches Tiger swing during practice and when it counts. Why? Because everyone, even Tiger Woods, needs someone to look past the obvious to help improve performance. Unfortunately, in the business of sales, rarely is there someone watching you perform. Therefore, It is important for you to seek out that special person, your very own swing coach. Having a good mentor can help alter your direction from the outhouse towards the penthouse. However, unless you are paying them the big bucks, it is imperative that you   treat them with R-E-S-P-E-C-T. They owe you nothing. Suffice it to say, it's harder to achieve greatness on your own rather than with the assistance of a coach. So, who's your Swing Coach?

"A lot of people have gone further than they ever thought they could because someone else thought they could."

1. ***Never Sacrifice Integrity:*** Clients first! Always do what is in the best interest of your clients,   never   your   commission, and never, ever do anything improper just to "close the deal." In the end, your reputation is everything. I call this integrity.

"If you have integrity, nothing else matters.
If you don't have integrity, nothing else matters!" [1]
~ Alan Simpson

---

1. Alan Simpson Quote approved for use by Mrs. Ann Pendley-Executive Assistant to Alan K. Simpson.

About Robert

If it's true "experience is the best educator," then having a person in your life with experience is possibly the next best thing.

Robert Goldsmith is a Financial & Sales coach, a speaker, a mentor and an entertaining trainer for business and marketing organizations.

If you were to trace Robert's history, you will find that his experience in finance dates back to 1978 (when he claims, "he was only 10"). With all those many years of experience, Robert is easily an extraordinary resource for anyone looking for assistance in financial planning or in search of guidance towards success.

As further evidence, Robert has often been featured in the *Los Angeles Daily News* as a financial advisor for current events, appeared in an infomercial on behalf of a nationwide financial assistance program, and has been interviewed on cable television for ideas on college funding. Additionally, Robert has been a spokesman for groups across the country including Cal-State University - Northridge, The Pennsylvania Foster Parent Society, as well as various financial advisor training events.

In the entertainment arena, Robert has appeared on the Television Show *Champion's The Competitive Edge,* and as a country dance professional in the 1993 instructional video: *Let's do some "Kountry Kickin,"* which is quite remarkable for the boy from New York City. He has also been interviewed on CBS News Radio and can occasionally be seen as the "sit-down" comic somewhere at an open-mike night or belting out *La Bamba* and *Love Potion Number 9* on Karaoke Nights.

Residing in both Los Angeles, CA and Dallas, TX, Robert is married to his lovely wife Deanna, his partner in business and in life. They have three kids, Adam, a college baseball official and recent graduate of San Diego State University, Samantha, the reigning 2014 Miss International and former 2013 Miss Texas International, and Cory, a College Baseball Pitcher, and student at University of Texas at Dallas. He has an affection for the *"Three B's"* - Baseball, Basketball and Bowling, both as a fan and an above-average participant and for always bringing laughter into the world, whenever and wherever he may be.

Soon to be featured on CNN, FOX and ABC, in addition to many other news outlets across the USA, Robert has been a licensed Insurance and Financial professional since 1982. He recently penned his own humorous book on sales and marketing success, *You're Earning What You Deserve... And That Sucks*. And, if that is not enough, his soon-to-be-released book on personal finance, *From Diapers to It Depends* ™ is already in the works.

Be sure to visit his websites at: www.RobertGoldsmith.org,
and: www.Financial411.net
or contact him via email at: Financial411@att.net.

If you are interested in developing a career in financial services or improving your current business, be sure to check out: www.AdvisorsIntegrity.com

CHAPTER 14

LET IT GO, LET IT GO

BY TOM SHIEH

It's funny how some distance
Makes everything seem small
And the fears that once controlled me,
can't get to me at all
It's time to see what I can do
To test the limits and break through
No right, no wrong, no rules for me
I'm free!
Let it go! Let it go!

~Elsa the Snow Queen
(from Disney's movie *Frozen* in the song *Let It Go!*)

Have you ever had something happen in the past that you just could not let go?

It's 2:46 am. I'm on international travel with my family, sitting on the floor in a corner of the room at one of the premier hotels in downtown Korea. It's a family vacation that we've planned for together for the greater part of this year. For months, my lovely wife researched which hotel we would stay at, what fun activities we would enjoy, and where we would go to explore. And because of our recent successes in various investment decisions, I told her to just book the absolute best.

I exclaimed, "Money isn't an issue, I will take care of it all!" As a man, it feels so incredibly good to be able to provide for your family in that manner.

However, as they are sleeping soundly in our luxurious room with plush beds, down pillows and comforters, my heart is not at peace and I cannot rest. I've been tossing and turning mentally, emotionally, and physically – not just tonight, but for days.

The truth is: I've been beating myself up as I've created a mental hell and placed myself right in the middle of it. I'm grieving a loss and I cannot seem to let go. From an emotional perspective, I'm not a suicidal person, but the pain gives me a glimpse into understanding how sometimes in a temporary moment, there can be a lapse in judgment during an emotional downswing without a strong mindset and compelling future.

A couple of months ago, the stock market provided some fascinating signals and indicators that I've waited patiently on for over a year. It was as if the markets were converging at a unique time through multiple confirmations. As a result, in a series of brilliant trades, I managed to make $250,000 in a short period of time. I was on Cloud Nine – feeling grateful, proud, guided, and enthusiastic. It was as if everything aligned for me, and with my trading and investment background, I was sophisticated and prepared to maximize the opportunity.

As the economic trend and patterns diverged, making the probability for success more unpredictable, I committed to myself that I would close out these positions, take the profits, and enjoy them fully.

After closing the positions as intended, I took my wife to Louis Vuitton, Apple, other fine stores. We celebrated with a little shopping to commemorate the victory. My wife and I are simple people, living contentedly with our basic necessities, as we don't need to have an extravagant lifestyle. However, it was a moment to remember for us.

The following day, we continued the celebration and joyfully shared with some select family members and also discussed how we would use those funds and give generously to charities, family members in need, and save a large portion for future purposes. I gave thanks to God publicly on Facebook and praised Him for His faithfulness in my life, as I realized the gains and closed out the positions.

I already mentally allocated all the money in my mind. I not only counted the eggs my chickens laid, but I envisioned those eggs hatching and creating more eggs, and counted all those as well. And I started to prepare accordingly.

The next day, following closing all the positions, I saw some additional opportunities to ride out some continuing trends. *One more trade* is I what I told myself, *just one more* and I'll stop. Well, I stopped alright. Within five more trades in what seemed to be a flash of time, all my profit was completely wiped out. What? Ouch! I was in shock and disbelief.

To put it in context, I could have bought a home for a family member with cash for a quarter of a million dollars. I could have paid for my kid's college education. I could have bought a nice car; in fact, I could have bought several cars. I could have gone on a cruise for 5 years in a row for a quarter of a million dollars. I could have started an orphanage or built a school. I could have given to my church and other charitable organizations. It was all gone now.

Oh, how I wish that I could be able to go back into that moment of time and make things right! However, fighting with reality only assures pain and frustration. When we live in past pains, it zaps our power and joy.

I was so disappointed and upset at myself that I was ashamed to share this with anyone; this was a big part of what ate me up alive. My wife and I have an extremely intimate relationship; we have shared everything together during our 20 years together. So, I refused to even tell her – as I couldn't stomach the thought of her loving, understanding, and empathetic reaction of caring on the surface, but knowing deep down that I'll have caused her unnecessary anxiety and heartache – not because of the money, but because of her love for me and how much she cares for me. When you love someone, their hurt becomes your hurt. So imagine when you're deeply in love with someone and their hurt becomes your hurt, which then becomes your hurt again, which becomes their hurt.

During these past few days, I realize on another level that the quality of our life is found in the quality of our inner dialog. The amplitude, tone, frequency, and context of that inner dialog will then determine our emotions. And, our emotions are nothing more than a shadow of our inner dialog; in other words, it's our thoughts that drive our emotions. Ultimately, our emotions are the filter of our human experience. And, my emotions have clouded that filter. That's why I have not been able to sleep at night. I cognitively knew it, but it was easier said than done.

My inner dialog began asking non-empowering questions over and over.

- Why were you so foolish?

- Do you know how disappointed your wife will be in you? You robbed your family.

- Don't you know that you're supposed to be a role model and inspiration for others?

- Why did you place that particular trade? Are you stupid?

- You never learn, do you? You knew better.

- Why did you commit to helping family members so generously? Now what?

- What could you have better spent that money on?

- What even riskier investment can you do to make all that

money back?

- Aren't you supposed to be good with money and investment principles?
- How are you supposed to pay for things now?
- Didn't you make a bunch of other bad decisions before?
- Why don't you just keep this to yourself for the rest of your life? Nobody needs to know.

The more that I tried to avoid asking these questions, the more this issue chased after me. The more that I tried to mute and block it out, the more amplified the emotions got. The more I resisted the hurt, the more it persisted.

I was clearly dwelling in the past, and because of it, I was creating a living hell for myself. Furthermore, I was preventing something better from coming forward. I was so tight-fisted with my pain that I was unwilling to open up my grasp to experience a greater gift. In our journey of growth, we are bound to experience disappointments. And when we experience these significant emotional events, there comes a point where we need to decide to spend our energy either hanging on to the past or to expend that energy on creating a greater future.

I reminded myself, "Let it go, Tom. Let it go!"

In a split moment of decision, I take leap of faith and courage. No more feeling sorry for myself! I took ownership of my thoughts, ownership of my internal dialog, ownership of the type of questions that I repeated to myself, and ownership in moving forward with greater wisdom and discernment. I sprang up off the hotel floor.

I intentionally run toward the very things that I was most afraid of instead of running away. I take massive action. That same evening, I write in my journal in a raw and unfiltered manner. While the kids were still sleeping, I share with my wife what was upon my heart as tears ran down my face. I decide that I would share this story in this book with others and release my fear of looking like a failure. Essentially everything that I was afraid of, I embraced. And because of it, the chains that once controlled me were broken.

It's amazing how a small decision and shift in attitude can create such a ripple effect. I became refocused, recharged, and invigorated. I went from being broken and hanging my shoulders to lifting up my head proudly and trusting that the best is yet to come. I went from feeling like a poor victim, to knowing in faith that I am guided and loved. It was a dramatic transformation. Upon returning from Korea, I get realigned and centered. I do what I'm good at and know. And in a matter of days, I make up that profit back again, and then some.

As I reflect back upon the experience, I believe there were five critical components that were tremendously helpful in that process of reclaiming my focus, energy, and perspective. They are vital essentials not only during the disappointments, obstacles, and challenges in life, but for everyday living. And as we look to experience explosive and sustainable growth and success, I commit to incorporate this as part of our daily regimen.

1. Decision

There's a difference between making a mental note and taking an active commitment decisively. While I was in the corner of that hotel floor, I decided once and for all that I was going to stop reliving the past pain. And, I was committed to letting it go and moving forward. It was done. I changed my posture from one of being defeated to one of someone who is victorious. I decided to stand differently. I decided to breathe differently. I decided to talk about the situation differently. And, I decided, once and for all, to think positively about the entire situation.

2. Expression

The source of depression can often be traced back to a lack of expression. When we bottle up our emotions, sentiments, and feelings, we suppress and depress our soul. During that restless evening in the hotel, I immediately grab my laptop and began journaling my thoughts, hurts, pains, and frustrations. I place all my emotions on paper instead of bottling it all in. It was raw.

There is such a freedom in expression. When we don't judge and condemn ourselves for how we feel, we give ourselves permission to release openly. I wrote and wrote for over 6 pages. Everything I could think of was released. In that process, I was able to shine a light into areas that I was trying to hide, conceal, and not face. As a result, I became truly liberated.

When there is true expression in our trials and hurts, the emotional charge naturally dissipates. When we resist, we choose to cling on to it. Until we fully express those emotions, the sticky residue that remains there haunts our soul.

3. Responsibility

A great way to look at the word responsibility is "response" + "ability". In other words, being responsible means having the ability to respond and to choose – being mindful in our circumstances and not being a victim. I decided that I was a victor, not a victim.

At any given moment, I have a choice. I have the ability to choose either feeling sorry for myself or to take responsibility for my own happiness. If we allow other people or external circumstances to dictate who we are or how we feel, our power is diffused.

I take responsibility for my life – my thoughts, my actions, and my response to life's circumstances.

4. Gratitude

One of the greatest ways to get centered and gain perspective is through gratitude. And, a great way to do that is through a series of empowering questions.

- What are you grateful for?
- What's beautiful about this?

- Who loves you? Who do you love?
- How can this serve you and build others up?

When we turn the eyes of our heart and mind toward the solutions to empowering questions, we immediately experience the joy of the things we focus upon. Our tears of pain become tears of joy. Our frowns become joyful smiles. For me, I envisioned my family – my wife, my kids, my brothers, my parents, and my community of loving friends. When we align ourselves through gratitude, doors and opportunities open up. When we look at things from a higher perspective of thankfulness, we realize the important things in our lives and our problems become smaller.

5. Forgiveness

Forgiveness is letting go. In this situation, there wasn't anybody that I was harboring resentment toward except myself. Forgiving ourselves can sometimes be even harder than forgiving others. I put down the club in which I was beating myself with. As achievers, we are often the most unkind to ourselves. Think about this thought:

Which is more unkind? The person or circumstance who offended us once or the person (ourselves) who repeats the story about the offense over and over again in their minds?

In my forgiveness, a giant weight was lifted off my shoulder. Because I forgave myself, there was no need to cling to the story that did not serve me well.

What about you? Is there anything that you need to let go and embrace?

Do yourself a big favor today. Let go of your past baggage. You have to let go of the past to enjoy the future you are dreaming of. Your journey will be much lighter and easier if you don't carry the pain with you. When we let go of the past, the past lets go of us. *Accept the lessons learned, allow them to teach you; but don't live in the past.*

Take a leap of faith and courage to face the areas that we are trying to run away from. Your soul will thank you for it. I assure you. You'll be amazed how you'll receive greater things that are in store for you.

About Tom

Tom Shieh is a partner of SmartMoney Financial Group and Turnkey Investment Fund, where he actively works with clients and strategic partners in unique investment opportunities not available to the general public.

In these private equity investment funds, their mission is to create an environment that allows them to translate their clients' values, goals, and beliefs into a custom-written financial strategy. Through this, their valued clients are able to achieve a day of complete financial independence as defined by the client. Each client has a custom financial strategy will includes specific actions needed on specific dates to create, accumulate, protect, and distribute their wealth in the most efficient manner. Ultimately, this clarity allows their clients the highest probability to achieve their goals for the reasons that are most important to them, while providing peace of mind throughout the entire process, until all their goals are achieved, regardless of what is going on in the economy.

Tom is a creative, serial entrepreneur with a Bachelor's Degree in Electrical Engineering and a Master's Degree in Telecommunications. Originally from Taiwan, he has several years of technical and management experience at IBM, Level 3 Communications, Northrop Grumman, and other top companies. His ability to find strategic solutions and opportunities in the marketplace accounts for the continued growth of his businesses.

Tom, a national speaker and best-selling author, has been quoted and featured in *Forbes Magazine* and on ABC, NBC, CBS, Fox television and website affiliates nationwide. He is extremely knowledgeable in various industries, having started and worked in over 13 businesses, and having built, managed, and acquired over 100+ revenue-generating websites in different niches.

In his spare time, he enjoys spending time with his wife and three kids, working out, playing the guitar, basketball, and is active in his church.

You can connect with Tom at:
Tom@SmartMoneyFinancialGroup.com
www.facebook.com/tomshieh
www.linkedin.com/in/tomshieh

CHAPTER 15

UNDERSTANDING THAT SUCCESS COMES FROM WHO YOU ARE, NOT WHAT YOU DO

BY GREG ROLLETT

We are taught from an early age to go to school, get good grades and the skills and education you receive will help you to get a good job. Then you are told to go to graduate school, get your doctorate, your MBA . . . all to help you advance your career.

But the advice they never tell you is to work on yourself, your personality, your relationships and to showcase who you are.

We focus on test scores and lab results. We then tie credential into credential and start adding letters to the back of our names. Next thing you know we are in the real world. Thrown to the wolves in the 'mean' streets of business.

And none of those credentials matter when it's you against the world. What matters is how you relate to the person on the other end of your conversation. How you connect. How you get in tune with their emotional needs at that specific moment in time. For all good business is done based on who we are, not necessarily what we do.

All doctors go to medical school. All pass state board exams. But not all doctors are created equal. They have different beliefs, different values, different systems and processes, different styles and different backgrounds.

Each factors into the acquisition and retention of a patient. And if you were a doctor, just relying on the fact that you have your shiny degree hanging on the wall, you are going to keep spinning around and around in circles losing clients to the new lowest price doctor with credentials.

I want you to focus on something much more important. I want you to focus on who you are . . . not what you do. And I want you to focus on the top of the food chain, not the bottom.

You see, today's affluent clientele are eager to work with people who are like them . . . who relate to them . . . who have an affinity or connection to their own life. They understand that most competent people with a certain skill level can perform the task at hand. What they really want is someone they know, like and trust.

They don't want an institution either. They want the person for the job. Remember those old mafia movies where someone would always shout out, "*I got a guy?*" You want to be that guy. Someone that gets referred. Someone that gets talked about at cocktail parties. Someone who is known for being the only solution for the given situation. Where no one else even comes up in conversation.

Different success and business mentors have made reference to this type of person before. They might be called a guru or wizard. Others might call them a savior or even an expert.

Legendary marketing and business strategist Jay Abraham has a brilliant strategy based around this theory called the Strategy Of Preeminence where you are seen as the most trusted advisor for life.

We call this person a Celebrity Expert®. It is someone who combines the marketing and "be seen everywhere" aura of a celebrity and the knowledge and talents of an expert. You see, being famous for being famous can only get you so far. You need to apply some type of skill or knowledge in order to take that fame and put it to good use.

Thus the Celebrity Expert knows that he needs to share his story of magic powers with the world. Much like how we know the origin stories of our comic book heroes like Superman and Spider-Man, so must everyone in your market know your story.

People remember these stories. I know people that can tell me the entire Bat-Man origin story and have never read one of his comics or seen any of the movies. That is the power of a great story that is told time and time again. It's about the person. There is an emotional connection to a boy whose parents are murdered and seeks vengeance.

Showcasing flaws is also a powerful part of the equation. It's ok to be vulnerable. To pull back the veil. Too often we showcase only the good. We try to manipulate perfect lives through social media. We post status updates only when vacationing in exotic locations or eating fine foods.

But a superhero without flaws ultimately becomes boring. We lose interest. We know what the outcome in going to be. The flaws give the character life. A reason to keep tuning in every week or month. Your own success depends on selling yourself, your personality and your own unique super powers.

YOUR STORY IS THE DRIVER OF NEW SUCCESS IN TODAY'S ECONOMY

Many entrepreneurs and professionals today simply have a fear of sharing their story. They fear they are not unique or distinctive. They feel their story is plain or boring.

171

That is simply not the case and is one of the biggest limiting beliefs to overcome. As humans we all relate on a very primitive level. Family. Travel. Hometowns. Love. Relationships. Food.

These build the essence of your story. . . where you grew up . . . how you grew up . . . the schools you went to . . . the sports teams you root for . . . your first love . . . your children. By starting on this basic level you start to create a connection that is easy for others to gravitate towards. It starts the conversation. And it continues the conversation.

It's the reason we go to the same barber for 20 years - we keep having that new conversation based on the connection we created the first time we sat in their chair.

It's the reason we go out of our way to the dentist who remembers us, has a child the same age as our own and always has a story to tell.

It's the reason we listen to certain news programs and sportscasters. The reason why we read every book from certain authors and never get into books from other authors. It's why we will watch certain movies before others - because of the story we heard about the actor or the filming of the movie - it's not just the movie itself.

We are drawn to people. And people working together provide the fastest path to success there is. One person sharing an idea with another person. An introduction or connection made. A partnership or joint venture opportunity. One person's resources being applied to another's ability to implement and act.

But none of this is possible without the two people getting together. And it's never the thing that gets them together. It's the two people connecting.

All too often we fall back on what we do. It's easy to talk about the details of the thing, the features, the benefits. It's harder to find stories and build context. But we remember the stories about the person and we forget facts. It's why 48% of all statistics are made up 63% of the time.

SO HOW CAN YOU FOCUS ON WHO YOU ARE AND NOT WHAT YOU DO?

By telling your story. And by using media to enhance the visibility of your story.

Every advertisement you write is a place to tell your story, not just what you do. Why do you do what you do? How did it come about? Where did your magic powers come from? What is the story about the first person that you helped?

These are all key elements to share every opportunity you can. It's why I lead every presentation, webinar, interview or video with some rendition of my background in the music industry, which led to starting my first business venture, which spawned my successful ventures today.

I do this for many reasons. The most prevalent is to have some common ground that people will want to talk to me about. It is something they will remember long after I leave the stage or the interview has ended.

They will remember that I was the marketing guy who used to be a rapper in a rock band. They will forget the facts, the tactics, the steps in whatever it is I am talking about. But they won't forget the fact that I was a musician, that I toured the country, that I survived on ramen noodles on the back of a van for weeks or that my band mates left me hanging out to dry just weeks after I got married to my high school sweetheart.

Do you see how I snuck all of that into this chapter?

And even with everything I have written about, it is those interesting tidbits about the author that you will remember above all else. My marketing skills are implied. You assume I can write a great sales letter or ad for you. You assume that I know my stuff. That I have the necessary credentials.

And it's the same in your business. The letters at the end of your name mean nothing to the person making the buying decision. And it will stop you from being successful in today's economy. It will hold you back. It is a belief you need to get over.

Today more than ever, you get paid and hired for who you are and not what you do. And the higher up the ladder of affluence you go, which is where you should be aiming at, the truer it becomes.

I was speaking with a client recently who was working on the marketing for his company. He said that his customers were having a hard time connecting to this product. They had the best specs, the best raw materials, the best formula, the best delivery times – everything you would want from this product.

The immediate problem I saw was that there was no human connection. All of the emails came from the institution. They sounded vanilla. There were no stories, just facts.

I reminded him that we forget facts. And we forget facts fast. But we remember people and stories. I told him to talk about his life. To introduce his daily thoughts and issues into his emails, newsletters and even proposals. I told him to start telling his story about why he started the company and the first customer he helped using his products. The minute he made that adjustment, the difference was clear. The customers had someone to cling onto. They suddenly remembered who he has when the phone rang. And when his sales reps went into the field they were flooded with questions about the CEO of the company and his kids, his trips around the world and about his magical powers.

Sales spiked because of stories, not specs. The specs were assumed at that point. They were a quick point of negotiation and reassurance as the contract was being signed.

Your business is too important to be forgotten. Especially in today's fickle economy. When price becomes a prospect's only point of reference, you lose. If you don't lose today, you will lose tomorrow. Someone will always come along cheaper and faster. But no one can replace you. Who you are. With the relationships and the connections that you have with your customers, your list, your clients.

The first step is to write down your story. Map it out. Reverse engineer the pieces that you want told and then re-told. Simplify the complicated. Create emotional ties. Paint pictures with your words.

After you have your story, start inserting it using media, both online and offline. In your brochures and catalogs, do you tell your story, the story behind the products, or do you just state the facts? If it's the facts, time to make a change.

In your social media posts are you just pointing people back to sales pages and product pages? Or are you connecting and sharing things about you? Make the change.

Most importantly, adapt the mindset that you are the biggest asset in your business. You alone have the ability to grow, multiply and expand your operation by sharing more of you. By telling your story and having others tell the tale for you. To build your legend. And it starts today. Your success depends on who you are, not what you do.

About Greg

Greg Rollett, @gregrollett, is a Best-Selling Author and Marketing Expert who works with experts, authors and entrepreneurs all over the world. He utilizes the power of new media, direct response and personality-driven marketing to attract more clients and to create more freedom in the businesses and lives of his clients.

After creating a successful string of his own educational products and businesses, Greg began helping others in the production and marketing of their own products and services. He now helps his clients through 2 distinct companies, Celebrity Expert Marketing and the ProductPros.

Greg has written for Mashable, Fast Company, Inc.com, the Huffington Post, AOL, AMEX's Open Forum and others, and continues to share his message helping experts and entrepreneurs grow their business through marketing.

Greg's client list includes Michael Gerber, Brian Tracy, Tom Hopkins, Coca-Cola, Miller Lite and Warner Brothers, along with thousands of entrepreneurs and small-business owners across the world. Greg's work has been featured on FOX News, ABC, NBC, CBS, CNN, *USA Today, Inc Magazine, The Wall Street Journal*, the *Daily Buzz* and more.

Greg loves to challenge the current business environment that constrains people to working 12-hour days during the best portions of their lives. By teaching them to leverage marketing and the power of information, Greg loves to help others create freedom in their businesses that allow them to generate income, make the world a better place, and live a radically-ambitious lifestyle in the process.

A former touring musician, Greg is highly sought after as a speaker, who has spoken all over the world on the subjects of marketing and business building.

If you would like to learn more about Greg and how he can help your business, please contact him directly at: greg@dnagency.com or by calling his office at 877.897.4611.